ALSO BY ANDRE M. PERRY

*Know Your Price: Valuing Black Lives and
Property in America's Black Cities*

BLACK POWER
SCORECARD

BLACK POWER SCORE-CARD

Measuring the Racial Gap and
What We Can Do to Close It

ANDRE M. PERRY

METROPOLITAN BOOKS

HENRY HOLT AND COMPANY   NEW YORK

Metropolitan Books
Henry Holt and Company
Publishers since 1866
120 Broadway
New York, New York 10271
www.henryholt.com

Library of Congress Cataloging-in-Publication data is available.

ISBN 9781250869715

Our books may be purchased in bulk for promotional, educational, or
business use. Please contact your local bookseller or the Macmillan Corporate
and Premium Sales Department at (800) 221–7945, extension 5442, or by
e-mail at MacmillanSpecialMarkets@macmillan.com.

First Edition 2025

Designed by Kelly S. Too

Printed in the United States of America

1   3   5   7   9   10   8   6   4   2

To my beloved Jade, Carlos, and Roby.
Strengthened by trials, we stand in power.

The first point was we wanted power to determine our own destiny in our own black community. And what we had done is, we wanted to write a program that was straightforward to the people.

—Bobby Seale

CONTENTS

Introduction   1

1. Not a Business Venture   17

2. Power to Live   28

3. Forty Acres and a Mall   49

4. Business-Built Black Power   71

5. Getting to Closing   96

6. Marriage Material   120

7. The Community as a Good School   137

8. Empowerment through Unity   160

9. Reparations Go to DC   178

Notes   201
Acknowledgments   225
Index   229

BLACK POWER
SCORECARD

INTRODUCTION

Not long ago, I received an email from the creators of the podcast *Black Politics Today* asking a basic question: "Black power—do we really have it?" On the face of it, the answer appears to be yes, we do.

"We are living in the time of a new renaissance—what we are calling the Black Renaissance," declared historian Ibram X. Kendi in a 2021 essay in *Time* magazine. He lauded the achievements of Black creatives in literature, film, music, theater, and the fine arts and proclaimed a cultural revival similar to the Harlem Renaissance in the 1920s and the Black Arts Movement in the 1960s and 1970s. Ava DuVernay, Cardi B, Jesmyn Ward, Michael B. Jordan, Alicia Garza—even if some people don't know their names, the prominence of these creators represents a palpable cultural shift, amplified by the racial reckoning that came in the aftermath of the 2020 murder of George Floyd. Black Lives Matter, one of the largest protest movements in history, peaked that year when half a million people participated in nearly 550 separate rallies throughout the country.[1] If the protests were prompted by the killings of unarmed Black people by the police, they were fueled by the grievance of untended claims of racial injustice across many realms of life.

The months of protests were seen as a further demonstration of power, illustrating the ability of Black Americans to convert tragedy and exhaustion into justice and recognition. Beyond this obvious strength to mobilize people, the calls for justice pushed corporate America to respond. The consulting firm McKinsey estimated that companies pledged $340 billion toward advancing racial equity between May 2020 and October 2022.[2] Then in April 2021, a jury sentenced former Minneapolis police officer Derek Chauvin to twenty-two and a half years in prison for killing Floyd; at the end at that year, Chauvin pleaded guilty to federal charges of violating Floyd's civil rights, resulting in an additional twenty-one-year sentence.

However, three years after Floyd's murder, the rate of police killings of Black people was unchanged, according to data compiled by the police reform organization Campaign Zero.[3] As Brookings senior fellow Rashawn Ray stated in a 2021 report, the "Chauvin trial was an exemplar" but "an outlier." It was "far from the norm of what typically happens when police use unjustifiable force and do not get convicted." And alongside the expansion of Black cultural influence, there has been a backlash. PEN America reported a significant increase in book bans, with 4,349 cases occurring across twenty-three states and fifty-two public school districts from July to December 2023.[4]

If the impact of the sweeping protests of 2020 and the

accomplishments of the cultural renaissance that Kendi identified are tenuous, how are we to assess Black power?

Power is broadly defined as the extent to which one can exert influence to achieve a desired outcome. But that definition doesn't fully capture its complexity or address the conflicting ideas of how power is acquired and how it should be exercised. Shifting views on power reflect changing cultural norms, underlying beliefs about human nature, visions of an ideal social order, and moral imperatives. The philosophical and cultural underpinnings that shape different conceptualizations of power inform the mechanics of gaining influence, the assumptions about what and who should be controlled, and ultimately what power looks like in real terms.

As with other conceptions of power, the idea of Black power emerges from a particular sociopolitical and economic context. From the twenty ministers who sought forty acres and a mule for every formerly enslaved family as a form of reparations at the close of the Civil War, to Fannie Lou Hamer fighting for voting rights in the 1960s, pivotal moments in Black people's efforts to gain freedoms and dignify their existence have defined Black power. Martin Luther King Jr. and Malcolm X mobilized communities for civil rights and economic justice, while Stokely Carmichael (Kwame Ture) popularized the term *Black Power*, operationalized by the Black Panther Party through its creation of direct service programs. These and similar events have unveiled core dimensions of Black power, distinguishing it within the broader landscape of power definitions.

Its essence is characterized by relentless efforts to exert

influence to secure basic democratic freedoms under the law and ensure that the principles enshrined in foundational documents such as the Constitution apply equally to all citizens. Black movements have consistently called for the recognition and advancement of cultural identity while fostering goals of self-determination and self-reliance. Through varied but interconnected activism, the struggle for Black power has been a persistent and evolving fight for justice and equity, while underscoring a deep commitment to both individual and collective empowerment. In all its stages, Black power uniquely offers an idyllic American vision of democracy and self-determination, a distinct landmark in the landscapes of power.

With the goal of securing substantive, concrete, and lasting power, this book articulates the objectives that can help lead to attaining it. Political scientists and organizers have explored the tactics used to achieve different ends, such as the civil rights movement's advocacy of nonviolence, including boycotts and marches, which comprise a Black tradition of action. However, this book focuses on aims, favoring objectives over strategies. Certainly, there are numerous kinds of progress that can empower a community, but which ones are pivotal for Black people? A construct of the ends of power must be understood and explicated if it is to be measured.

Black Power Scorecard uses data to identify the key goals necessary for expanding and securing power, which help set priorities, such as increasing homeownership, for example, over winning Oscar or Grammy awards, or investing in Black-owned businesses rather than creating conditions to enlarge the number of Black billionaires. This book aims to create a hierarchy of indicators of power that, if addressed, would enhance Black people's influence and ability to achieve other goals that are ranked lower in the hierarchy. *Black Power Scorecard* will demonstrate why prioritizing homeownership can in fact lead to winning more Grammys, laying out the strategic focus on empowering the Black community broadly and effectively.

Some deliberately equate Black power with White Power, a slogan frequently heard at white supremacist gatherings and even at certain presidential rallies.[5] The slogan, intended to parallel the Black power movement, suggests that the calls for white power seek reasonable empowerment goals akin to the aims of Black people. Alternatively, it's cited to argue that Black power is just as discriminatory as the white version. Following this logic, detractors liken Black Lives Matter protesters to white extremists and terrorists, misrepresenting the movement's call for racial justice and equality.

To be clear, White Power is a slogan of white supremacy, a framework of power built on the belief that "white people constitute a superior race and should therefore dominate society, typically to the exclusion or detriment of other racial and ethnic groups."[6] White supremacy seeks to install privileges based on a racial hierarchy, while Black power seeks to remove privileges based on race. White power is inherently antidemocratic, while the rise of Black power would advance democracy, benefiting all racial groups.

The quest to secure Black power is not and should not be understood as a mission to emulate white power or simply to gain access to white institutions. In their attempts to spotlight inequality, people often cite comparisons to white society in ways that tacitly reinforce white norms and standards. An example of this is when Jay-Z called out the Grammys for failing to honor Beyoncé with its highest prize, the Album of the Year award. Doing so helped reinforce the notion that white culture, white identity, and white-centric institutions are the standards or norms that others are expected to follow.[7] White normativity is fundamentally about power and its invisibility, underscoring the privilege of whiteness to establish such standards. Anthropologist Gloria Wekker argues that white norming creates a "racial grammar" that shapes thoughts, effects, and even individual self-perceptions, in a profound cultural archive that inherently favors whiteness.[8] This dynamic enables white individuals to assume positions of invisibility and superiority, perpetuating a standard by which whiteness is the benchmark of humanity such that deviation from this norm is seen in racialized terms.

While the Recording Academy is not a "white institution" per se, its development has been white-centric, and it has a long way to go before becoming a truly multicultural organization in which racial bias doesn't have a negative impact on its subjective valuations. More important, winning more Grammys isn't going to move the needle on increasing Black wealth.

Still, influencing cultural institutions is nonetheless important to power building because institutions shape narratives about the human condition. All sponsors of art explicitly or implicitly color our notions of what constitutes high and low culture, how it looks, sounds, and smells, and these notions shape public policy. The harmful effects of demonizing Blackness were powerfully demonstrated in the famous doll test, in which Black children, presented with similar Black and white dolls, identified the Black dolls as "ugly and bad."[9] By exposing that harm, the test helped plaintiffs win the landmark 1954 Supreme Court case *Brown v. Board of Education of Topeka*, which overruled the "separate but equal" doctrine that had legally enshrined segregation. Through such efforts and through art and culture, in books like Toni Morrison's *The Bluest Eye*, society has come to see the inherent value bestowed on whiteness and the burdens assigned to Blackness that undergird social policy.

In the context of seeking recognition and representation within predominantly white institutions, assimilation is not inherently a goal or an indicator of Black power, given the problematic dynamics involved. While the historical struggle for equality has aimed to eliminate the bias and discrimination that hinder assimilation, the process of assimilation often involves compromising dignity and stripping away important, often immutable, aspects of one's identity—that is, whitewashing. The ubiquitous practice in professional life, especially in entertainment, requiring people to straighten their hair to mimic white styles is a glaring example. (Thankfully, CROWN Act legislation, which prohibits hair discrimination, is being passed across the country.)

However, whitewashing does reveal the intrinsic and material advantages of whiteness. Black homeowners, for example, can increase the worth of their property—adding thousands in actual value—by replacing Black art, books, clothing, and hair products with items that signal white ownership. In 2020, the *New York Times* reported on a Jacksonville, Florida, couple whose home yielded a 40 percent higher appraisal value after they whitewashed it.[10] That same year, an Indianapolis woman did the same and enlisted a white stand-in, boosting the appraisal by $134,000.[11] One Black homeowner, who gained some $300,000 in value after whitewashing her home, told me that she feared the appraiser was on to her when she left a jar of cocoa butter on the dresser.

There are those who see emulation as the path to Black power, expressed as needing to "do what the opposition does" and out of a desire to adopt the same playbook used to discriminate against Black people. This eye-for-an-eye strategy runs the risk not only of dehumanizing those who use it, but also of replicating the outcomes with which Black people currently live.

My research makes it clear, for example, that being better capitalists will not significantly advance the Black community's socioeconomic status. There is a complex relationship between Black power and economic empowerment, but individual wealth, exemplified by Black billionaires, does not inherently translate to collective advantage. It may even reinforce racial and economic hierarchies.

Acclaim from mainstream institutions, assimilation, whitewashing, and emulation will not provide the flex that gives Black people the capital and influence they need. Nor will achieving parity in prestigious awards. This will not restore the home value that's been denied by racism or increase homeownership, which point to a truer assessment of Black power. The metrics by which we should measure Black power and the goals we must set to achieve it involve advocating away from individual achievements and toward collective progress and well-being.

In the new renaissance, the Black Americans who write the stories, sing the songs, cook the food, and dribble the basketballs are demanding sovereignty and ownership: they seek their own platforms to show their full humanity and establish new lines of authority. They seek to build institutions that hire employees who are paid a living wage. They are engaged in activities that build up communities rather than exploit them. Thus rapper Killer Mike, Ambassador Andrew Young Jr., and media executive Ryan Glover cofounded Greenwood, a mobile banking platform inspired by Black Wall Street, which flourished in the early 1900s Greenwood district in Tulsa, Oklahoma. Cultural leaders are building venues, organizations, and bodies of work that heighten their control and commercial value.

The names Kendi cites in his *Time* essay aren't just a Black History Month roster (the month of recognition has itself become a racist trope) or a rattled-off list of successful people. While he acknowledges the brilliance of the work of producer-actor Issa Rae, director Regina King, performer Billy Porter, writer Jason Reynolds, and others, his point is that the power of their artistry comes from a newfound capacity to set self-defined cultural standards, ones that are driven by the ways in which Black creatives experience humanity and are free from the burden of fulfilling white norms. In the same way, the expansion of Black power and the metrics we use to assess it requires setting self-defined material and communal standards, free from the markers of success prescribed by others.

* * *

THE ULTIMATE EXPRESSION of power is surely the ability to live a full, natural life, so the first metric, preceding all others, is longevity, which depends on safety and access to resources. Situating Black power within this ultimate indicator, life expectancy, economist Jonathan Rothwell and I have examined how various social determinants—wealth, homeownership, education, and the built environment—contribute to safety and well-being and affect Black longevity. Instead of comparing Black to white people, we examined life expectancy and well-being differences among the Black population in a range of places, moving away from the Black-white disparity frame.

We noted hundreds of places that exceed commonly held expectations in the Black Progress Index, an interactive tool and report developed in partnership with the NAACP that provides a means to understand the health and well-being of Black people and the conditions that shape their lives.[12] This method revealed the locales where Black people are thriving. Using a regional approach allowed us to identify place-based strengths and needs, and to see different degrees of power development in diverse areas to quantify the key components of a long life. We were also able to measure the absence of these components.

The continuous struggle of African Americans toward self-determination and economic freedom is closely linked to ownership. The positive impact of business and real estate ownership on life expectancy within Black communities not only highlights the inherent power of ownership as a means to achieve the long-standing goal of self-reliance, it enhances life itself. While being a better capitalist is not an inherent goal of Black power, business ownership is a significant indicator. The story of Black entrepreneurship is deeply interwoven with the pursuit of racial equality and justice, and it is about more than making money: it represents a challenge to systemic barriers inherited from a history of exclusion and exploitation. It is also a testament to Black resilience, innovation, and ingenuity, given the obstacles that must be overcome to start and maintain a business. Clearing those hurdles and leveraging opportunities in industries, from health care to real estate development, not only paves the way for personal success but also contributes to the economic empowerment of the larger Black community. Additionally, by chronicling the resurrection of a once thriving retail hub, we were also able to assess the potential impact of collective economic action.

Another powerful indicator of longevity is homeownership—the data I explore in this book reveals a strong correlation between the two: a higher percentage of Black homeowners in an area correlates with longer life expectancies. This relationship underscores the profound impact of property ownership on wealth accumulation, political representation, economic growth, and, crucially, health outcomes. Bridging the homeownership gap is therefore a critical foundation for gaining Black power as well as a tangible measure of success and stability. That gap is considerable: in the fourth quarter of 2023, the homeownership rate among non-Hispanic white Americans was 73.8 percent, followed by Asian Americans at 63 percent, Hispanic Americans at 49.8 percent, and Black Americans at 45.9 percent.[13] This book advocates for innovative approaches and policies that remedy systemic obstacles and promote equitable access, among them special purpose credit programs, automatic refinancing, and new collective ownership models. Increasing homeownership to life-enhancing levels will require collective action and systemic change to realize the full potential of homeownership.

Family structure is related to power, and with it the assumption that parenting, specifically two-parent households, lays the foundation for individual, family, and community growth. I inspect the complex dynamics of marriage within the Black community and examine the far-reaching impact of systemic inequalities on family structures. Marriage can be an important power-building tool, but we need to focus more on the systemic barriers that discourage Black people from marrying, rather than on interpersonal social and emotional dynamics, which distract from the causal reasons why Black people marry less than they would in the absence of racism.

Of course, there are powerful links between education, Black empowerment, and longevity. Access to and quality of schooling play transformative roles in shaping life choices and opportunities, and disparities in education directly correlate with economic disadvantages and higher incarceration rates, which disproportionally affect the Black community. As I argue, wealth predicts educational outcomes, not the other way around. Therefore we must create the conditions for educational growth by enriching the neighborhoods in which schools sit and students live. Crucially, the Black Progress Index shows that performance on math tests by county is a strong predictor of life expectancy. Access to quality teachers and curricula is vital, but studying doesn't start and end in the classroom. We must go beyond the schoolhouse to create opportunities for learning, along with employment and ownership.

Income levels are also pivotal to establishing power. Higher incomes are strongly connected to increased life expectancy, leading to healthier, longer lives—a truism recognized by both researchers and ordinary people. I argue that a revitalized union movement is the most effective means of ensuring wages that will cover a family's basic needs where they live.[14] Unionization is the fundamental strategy for enhancing the socioeconomic status of Black workers.

All these measures add up to one of the oldest aims of the movement to achieve Black power: securing the foundational capital to thrive in America. Systemic racism has denied Black Americans the capital, land, and wages that are owed to them. Following the Civil War, the Freedmen's Bureau ultimately failed to provide reparations for slavery to protect long-term wealth building, and all subsequent efforts to remedy the damage caused by discrimination have been thwarted. The result of that discrimination, endorsed by federal, state, and local governments, can be seen and felt in a wealth gap whereby the average white family has roughly 6.7 times the wealth of the average Black family. Consequently, calls for reparations for these harms have never gone away.

When aldermen in Evanston, Illinois, approved the country's first municipal reparations program, it drew criticism, and not just from people who hate the very idea of reparations. "I am 100 percent in support of reparations," said Cicely Fleming, the lone alderman who voted against the measure, which plans to spend an initial $400,000 on housing grants of $25,000 each to Black residents to cover mortgage costs, down payments, and home improvements. "But what is before us tonight is a housing plan dressed up as reparations."[15] Another criticism by advocates of reparations holds that a mere housing program will rob momentum from more sweeping efforts at the federal level. "True reparations only can come from a full-scale program of acknowledgment, redress and closure for a grievous injustice," argued A. Kirsten Mullen and William A. "Sandy" Darity Jr. in a *Washington Post* op-ed.[16]

I will dig deeply into the topic of reparations in the context of environmental injustice caused by toxic industrial sites, using as a case study the initiative in Houston, Texas, to relocate residents away from polluted neighborhoods. While not explicitly labeled "reparations" by city officials, the proposal recognizes tacit responsibility by local government for perpetuating environmental injustice and seeks to address it through concrete measures. Houston's remedial action serves as an implicit model of local reparations and signifies a growing awareness and acknowledgment of past injustice at a municipal level, paralleling broader calls for reparations across the nation. These calls span various states and are aimed at addressing historical wrongs, including slavery, segregation, and discrimination, that have left a lasting impact on Black Americans.

This is by no means an exhaustive list of goals for Black power movements, but securing land and property for suitable means of production and business, building strong families, obtaining quality education, earning a livable wage, attaining homeownership, living in a clean environment, and winning reparations represent the most influential elements of life outcomes. These goals are familiar and have been pursued for generations, but here their pursuit is validated empirically. They continue to provide clear direction at a time when the tools and tactics used to promote racial justice have been under attack.

In the landmark 2023 ruling *Students for Fair Admissions, Inc. v. President and Fellows of Harvard College*, the US Supreme Court struck down race-based affirmative action in college admissions. The Supreme Court ruled that Harvard College and the University of North Carolina had violated the Equal Protection Clause of the Fourteenth Amendment and Title VI of the Civil Rights Act of 1964 by employing admissions processes that intentionally discriminated against Asian American applicants based on their race and ethnicity.[17] As a result, the court mandated that universities cease using race as a factor in future undergraduate admissions decisions. The ruling also requires that the process be conducted in a manner that prevents those involved in making decisions from knowing the race or ethnicity of any applicant.

The Supreme Court's decision has opened the door to questions of whether similar legal arguments can be made under related laws, specifically Title VII of the 1964 Civil Rights Act, which addresses employment discrimination, and Section 1981, derived from the post–Civil War 1866 Civil Rights Act, which ensures that certain rights previously exclusive to white individuals, including the rights to make contracts and own property, apply to all US citizens. Scholars at the Stanford Center for Racial Justice believe that the court might well apply the same reasoning to these statutes as it did in the *Students for Fair Admissions* case. This precedent has encouraged those who have challenged affirmative action policies to also target newer diversity, equity, and inclusion (DEI) programs and initiatives.

DEI, affirmative action, and environmental, social, and governance programs represent institutional responses to the mobilization and organization efforts of Black communities. But these tactics and tools are not the ultimate goals. The concepts, strategies, and objectives of Black power have never been fully encapsulated by such programs. The true endpoint has always been securing the means to ensure long lives and well-being. Tactics will change, but Black power must be gained alongside racial justice to increase longevity and provide restitution.

NOT A BUSINESS VENTURE

"What's better than one billionaire?"

In the 2019 song "Family Feud," rapper and mogul Jay-Z asks the question over a hard beat and rapturous, choral melodies provided by his wife, Beyoncé. The rapper, who famously said he was not a "businessman" but a "business, man" and bragged that he could sell water to a whale, answers, "Two," adding, especially if they're "from the same hue as you."

With these few lines, Jay-Z advances a slippery but commonly held theory that Black power will primarily be gained through private enterprise and wealth building. He preaches this gospel, a gospel of Black individuals' accumulation of riches for themselves and their families, in a music video set in a Baptist church. He also urges his fans to stop him rapping when he stops telling the truth. Full stop.

Standard record contracts, which require artists to pay back cash advances based on a small fraction of their sales, put most musicians in perpetual indebtedness, not too dissimilar in structure from a system of indentured servitude. Few become wealthy; many remain subservient to a company. This is standard fare in how a billion is made in the music industry, which didn't invent the model. Cheap and free labor facilitated by many industries fueled the country's rise as an economic power, with slavery being the most egregious example. Having a Black slave owner, or even two, would not have been better for Black communities. Nor is a billionaire, or even two.

Ignoring how a billion is made palliates the exploitation that is often required to make large sums of wealth. Sociologist Manning Marable made the case plainly in his classic *How Capitalism Underdeveloped Black America*. "Capitalist development has occurred not in spite of the exclusion of Blacks, but because of the brutal exploitation of Blacks as workers and consumers," Marable wrote. Racism has always been a key ingredient in the recipes for profit in industries such as insurance, banking, manufacturing, farming, and music. And for almost as long as that perverse production function has been around, so has the art of persuading Black Americans to accept exploitation, which involves convincing them that they can emulate the same practices that propelled wealth and power among white people.

When I started talking to researchers, leaders, and everyday people about measuring Black power, many of them referenced business successes. In particular, they cited the Black people, among them many entertainers, on the *Forbes* World's Billionaires List. Business development is indeed a gauge of power, but any assessment has to go beyond that limited value.

People are not businesses. They don't live in corporate offices. (If they do, they're probably in need of therapy.)

People live fully in communities and neighborhoods. They have families. People are loving, educable, communal, spiritual beings whose lives are not calculable as commodities. Consequently, we need a different framework to measure power, one that captures our full selves.

Historically, Black power movements fought for economic empowerment and encompassed business development, but many, like Marable, understood an exclusive capitalistic frame to be a flawed approach. Nonetheless, the free enterprise doctrine has become so ubiquitous that its limits warrant articulating. The elevation of free enterprise has served to devalue critical social, political, and cultural aspects of power building. At worst, its application extinguishes the efforts of people who don't have the capital to engage with financial power brokers. The rights of landlords are generally valued more highly than those of their tenants.

During an appearance in which Jay-Z talked about his company's partnership with the NFL, he was asked about Colin Kaepernick, the professional quarterback the league blackballed in 2016 for taking a knee during the national anthem to protest police brutality. Jay-Z stated, "I think we've moved past kneeling. I think it's time for action." Civil disobedience does not, it seems, count as "action" to Jay-Z.

Snubbing civil disobedience, as well as government programs, as part of a more comprehensive approach to power building is why *Black capitalism*, the post–civil rights movement that sought to empower Black people primarily through business development, mostly failed Black people since President Richard Nixon promoted it in the late 1960s. While Nixon endorsed Black participation in free markets, he rebutted calls for reparations and government redress. In their place he offered tax breaks and other fiscal incentives, the devices that power wealth. "Instead of government jobs and government housing and government welfare," Nixon said in a speech, "let government use its tax and credit policies," to power "the greatest engine of progress ever developed in the history of man: American private enterprise."[1]

But for Black people, centuries of discriminatory public policies profoundly constrained wealth generation and the power that goes with it. Being denied housing, employment, and other opportunities—such as low-interest loans, mortgages, and the investments in infrastructure that facilitated the rise of the white middle class in the postwar era—means that Black Americans have less capital with which to participate in the capitalist system. Therefore utilizing other forms of power becomes absolutely necessary if we want change. Individual wealth building and business development are certainly critical components of an empowerment agenda for Black people in America, but they're a feeble substitute for a comprehensive framework and a collective approach.

A better economic metric that serves as a reasonable proxy for power in a capitalist society is median wealth, which measures the average family's ownership of homes, businesses, and health insurance policies, and their student and medical debt. The median wealth or net worth of Black Americans conveys the overall material resources the community can enlist to influence change. It's a measure of collective power. According to the Federal Reserve, in 2022, the median net worth of Black families was $44,890, while that of white families was $285,000, 6.7 times greater.

Closing that gap depends to some extent on enlarging the share of Black-owned businesses to increase power and wealth. Business ownership represents about 10 percent of Black wealth compared to 17 percent of the white population's wealth. In 2021, Black people represented 14.4 percent of the population but owned only 2.7 percent of employer firms, that is, businesses with more than one employee. If the share of Black employer firms matched or surpassed the Black population percentage, as it does among white and Asian populations (72.5 percent and 6.3 percent of the US population, respectively, with 82 percent and 10.9 percent of employer firms), the economy would increase by 682,000 businesses and hundreds of billions of dollars. Still, with that boost, increasing the share of Black employer firms would not close the wealth gap.

The reason business ownership is a small piece of collective Black net worth is due to a lack of overall wealth. Most people start their businesses, for example, with equity they've accrued by owning their home. In 2021, Black homeownership stood at 46.4 percent, compared to 75.8 percent for white families. Disparities in homeownership mean fewer Black businesses. Thus inflating the significance of business ownership minimizes other important aspects of power building, such as creating federal policies aimed at increasing Black homeownership.

As economist William Darity Jr. stated in a 2021 *New York Times* editorial, "The sheer size of the wealth gap requires massive federal intervention to close it, and justice requires that the U.S. government fulfill its unmet obligations to African American slaves and their descendants."[2] The racial disparity among employer firms is a problem stemming from the wealth gap, rendering employment an insufficient solution for closing it.

Moreover, the racial wealth gap was generated by discrimination baked into federal, state, and municipal policies that prohibited wealth development. Since the early 1800s, talented businesspeople such as William Alexander Leidesdorff (merchant and warehouser), John Carruthers Stanly (former slave who ran a barbering company), Jeremiah Hamilton (broker), and Madam C. J. Walker (purveyor of cosmetics and hair care products) proved that Black individuals could certainly grow fortunes, despite the architecture of white racism. However, their rise is not cleanly associated with Black power.

John Stanly purchased the freedom of more than a dozen enslaved people, including members of his family, but he also purchased slaves to help run his barbering business and work his North Carolina plantation, which produced cotton and turpentine. At the height of Stanly's wealth, he was one of the largest slave owners in Craven County. However, being a member of the slave owner club did not prevent Stanly's downfall. He cosigned a bank loan issued to his half brother, who defaulted on it, bringing his ascent to a crashing end. With his land and property seized and sold by the sheriff, Stanly, once a powerful entrepreneur, died with the same amount of assets as the people he enslaved.

Stanly's example might be remote, but it is instructive as a lesson in the harm of adopting strategies that exploit

Black labor, talent, and resources—the foundations of economic and community growth. It is ultimately self-defeating to extract from the people and resources that are needed for a thriving community. The exploitation of people and their labor erodes a society's overall well-being, a society in which the exploiter often lives.

The New Economics Foundation provides a succinct definition of well-being, which encompasses the social, economic, and political factors that shape our experience: "Well-being can be understood as how people feel and how they function, both on a personal and a social level, and how they evaluate their lives as a whole."[3] One component of this is longevity, which is plainly measured by life expectancy. Well-being and longevity offer evidence that members of entire communities are empowered; these metrics complement median wealth to offer a better economic expression of Black power. Beyond money and individual gains, the impact of a person's successes is also composed of the value they add to their overall lives and to the communities in which they reside.

As a Black slave owner, Stanly amassed wealth that was a significant form of power, but he was still a Black man in a racist society. He was unable to prevent foreclosure or negotiate with the institutions that seized his assets. Power that is singularly tethered to an individual's money or wealth is tenuous and vulnerable.

Promoting business ownership as a primary strategy for power building is inadequate in other ways. For one, it fails to address the unequal advantage of those who have already largely gained capital. The wealthy don't have to start businesses to maintain their lead. White oligarchs have historically used discrimination and the exploitation of labor to build assets and wealth, and they continue to do so. They also use tax policy and investments to grow their capital. As the rates of return on capital exceed overall economic growth, including the economic returns from labor, it becomes harder for anyone with a dollar and a dream to compete. The rich get richer by the dint of their existing capital and privilege.

Additionally, some forms of value cannot be measured by economic standards. Much of what we understand as Black power grew out of Black people seeing value in "assets" ignored by traditional markets. The value of Black people's homes, traditions, and businesses well exceeds the prices that are placed on them. Historically, much of our power emanated from resisting the frameworks and methods that have exploited talent, culture, and facets of well-being. Black music offers a great example.

In 1725, in its Louisiana territory, France implemented Le Code Noir, which, among other rules, established Sunday as a day of rest for enslaved Africans in New Orleans. On Sundays, Black people, who originated from various African countries, would congregate, share information, and form markets where they would buy and sell their goods throughout the parish, often saving up enough to buy their freedom. Shortly after the United States acquired the territory through the Louisiana Purchase in 1803, city officials restricted the day of rest to one specific area: Congo Square, a 4.5-acre area where enslaved and free people of color would gather to worship, organize, exchange goods, sing, dance, and find moments of joy in an overarching environment of oppression. Congo Square birthed the sound of jazz, the product of Black people's collective efforts to thrive.

Over the past century, jazz has powered record companies, clubs, other art forms, and social movements. As *New York Times* music critic Giovanni Russonello wrote in 2021, "As it evolved, jazz remained a resistance music precisely because it was the sound of Black Americans building something together, in the face of repression."[4] Blues, rhythm and blues, and hip-hop are the offspring of jazz, and each genre passed on capacities to help Black communities grow.

There are certainly entrepreneurs and practices that do add value and enhance power. But the racial wealth gap cannot be closed by Black participation in free enterprise alone. It will be closed only by eliminating systemic racism and restoring the equity that has been extracted from Black Americans in many sectors, through such programs that can be broadly considered as reparations. In this book, I argue for redress for racial discrimination in areas other than slavery. However, the creation of a congressional act that provides reparations for the atrocities of slavery and the depredations that followed will mean that Black people have gained sufficient power—politically, socially, economically, and culturally—to make that happen.

Still, the centuries-old call for reparations is inherently an appeal for a fuller conceptualization of power building than a narrow focus on business development can provide. Measurements of Black power must consider *wealth*, *human and social capital* (e.g., education, social networks, religion), *environmental quality*, *safety*, and *family*. The multiple facets of Black well-being are cheapened by individualistic notions of Black power. To get beyond distracting notions of bootstrapping entrepreneurs, we must internalize and operationalize Black power as inherently collective in nature.

There is an African proverb that says, "If you want to go fast, go alone. If you want to go far, go together." We must measure the distance that Black people must travel collectively to have greater influence on the conditions that affect longevity and prosperity. It's at the collective scale that we can grasp how much progress we have made and the magnitude of the solutions needed to gain Black power.

* * *

"ARE BLACK PEOPLE making progress in the United States?" is a question frequently posed to pundits and experts. Largely due to the framing of the close-ended, yes/no question, responses often compare current conditions to times of de jure segregation and discrimination.

"Blacks today are more likely to experience group preferences than racial slights, and they have the legal recourse when discrimination does occur," wrote Black conservative Jason L. Riley in his 2017 book *False Black Power*, intimating that progress had been made. After showing that people ought to see certain statutory changes as unquestionable signs of progress, Riley shifts blame for racial disparities from policy to people. "In the 1960s black people risked life and limb to cast a ballot," Riley added.[5]

Riley's claim didn't age well. Debased policymaking around voting rights prior to the 2020 presidential election made clear that Black voters are still endangered. As many Republican officials promulgated Donald Trump's lies after the election, they worked in state legislatures across the country to create the conditions that would allow them to suppress votes to win future elections. In Georgia, Governor Brian Kemp signed into law a bill that added many obstacles to voting, including reducing the number of ballot boxes, shrinking the window for early voting, adding photo ID requirements, and allowing state officials to circumvent the work of county election officials if they don't like the outcomes they are seeing.[6] The Georgia bill went so far as to make it illegal for outside groups to give water or food to voters stuck in long lines.

Riley's simplistic comparisons to a segregated past serve to dismiss the existence and profundity of current policies that generate negative outcomes for Black people. Pointing to statutory changes to de jure segregation also facilitates vapid, absolutist pronouncements. "There aren't any more excuses," is one, which removes the responsibility for confronting racially biased policies such as three-strike laws, appraisal bias, and tilted school financing systems. When policy is removed from consideration, there is nowhere to go but to blame Black people and to cast individual behaviors as the true enemy of progress. Calls for personal responsibility naturally follow. In fact, progress is not a yes/no proposition. Black people can't possibly shoulder all the blame for outcomes. We need a more useful framework to measure progress and power, one that encompasses all the structural and behavioral factors that influence family and community well-being.

2

POWER TO LIVE

"Like anybody, I would like to live a long life—longevity has its place. But I'm not concerned about that now. I just want to do God's will."[1]

Martin Luther King Jr. uttered these eerily prophetic words on April 3, 1968, the eve of his assassination. While pursuing economic rights for Black sanitation workers in Memphis, King reached the point at which he was willing to forgo his own longevity to work for that of others. His recognition of his vulnerability highlighted the fact that power is ultimately expressed through life itself. The ability to live out one's natural life depends greatly on the power associated with basic safety as well as political and economic rights, which pave the way for good schools, quality housing, jobs that pay a living wage, health care, and strong families. In its purest form, Black power is about being able to expect to live a long life.

Black people need power that is restorative in nature, to add quality and years of life through cooperation, resource sharing, and coordination. King also said, "We adopt the means of nonviolence because our end is a community at peace with itself." Similarly, power building must embrace longevity, safety, self-control, and rest.

Having in mind the goal of a peaceful community as we seek to measure power, we should look toward geographic areas where Black people are living the longest, because longevity reflects personal behaviors as well as the policy decisions that influence the quality of one's life. Assuming that individuals make decisions that add value to their lives, the places where people are living the longest provide insights into the efficacy of civic actions that increase longevity.

Cities and neighborhoods store past and present policy decisions that have a bearing on the life course of Black residents. Systems of enslavement that exploited African Americans were built upon the environmental destruction of land once inhabited by Indigenous people. Those systems evolved: as plantations were replaced by factories, many of the same neighborhoods and families experienced increased exposure to environmental pollutants. Infrastructure and housing policies tended to make situations worse, segregating Americans of color into more degraded environments, bisecting Black communities with dirty highways, and restricting opportunities for Black people to access green spaces. Places are not neutral. Black people's choices are contained in neighborhood contexts of biased policy, reflected by lower life expectancy than their white and Asian peers.

In 2019, life expectancy at birth for Black people was 74.8, which is lower than all other major race and ethnic groups except American Indian and Alaska Natives (71.8). Non-Hispanic white Americans have a life expectancy of

78.8, while Latino or Hispanic and Asian American life expectancies are 81.9 and 85.6, respectively.[2]

However, these national averages mask very real progress in Black America that is reflected in higher life expectancies at the local level. There are places in which Black people are exceeding national averages and predictions. In Manassas Park, Virginia, and Weld County, Colorado, the mean life expectancy for Black residents is ninety-six—a national high among all Black citizens by county.[3] Black people are living into their eighties in larger Democratic jurisdictions like Montgomery County, Maryland, and smaller Republican districts like Collier County, Florida. Yet in Jefferson County, Ohio, the average Black person lives thirty-three fewer years than the national high. That gap mirrors the kinds of improvements in living standards, medical science, and public health that accrued over the last one hundred years.

Life expectancy summarizes the biological and nonbiological factors, including racist policies, that influence a person's life. Because race is a sociological construct and not a biological one, we should assume disparities in life expectancy represent differences in nonbiological influences on our lives. Social determinants—neighborhood conditions shaped by social policy and behaviors—add or subtract years of life. Differences in social determinants have much to do with variations in civic actions of the people in those locales. Consequently, some Black people are winning battles against structural racism, while others are being hurt by it.

The social determinants represent crucial leverage points of power, which also offer an organizing framework for community and policy leaders. Power hinges on the extent to which people can maximize or minimize these determinants. This chapter elucidates the most influential social determinants of life expectancy that need to be addressed to optimize Black people's lives and power in distinct geographic regions. The chapters that follow explore the factors that would increase life expectancy for Black people, with the goal of reaching the top percentile overall, approximately eighty-three years. So how does one determine which factors are most important for longevity?

For the Black Progress Index, we ran hundreds of variables from a variety of data sources through a common machine-learning algorithm (Lasso) to find the most influential social determinants on life expectancy. Sources included databases from the US Census Bureau, Internal Revenue Service, Federal Reserve, Facebook, Redfin, the US Congress Joint Economic Committee's Social Capital Project, the County Health Rankings and Roadmaps program, and the Centers for Disease Control and Prevention (CDC). Although thousands of positive and negative factors influence life expectancy, we landed on thirteen variables that differentiated themselves by their significance: the rate of Black homeownership; college attainment; median household income; the rate of business ownership; mean distance from Facebook friends; foreign-born share of Black adults; air pollution; commute via bike or walking; math achievement among public-school students; church membership per capita; population density; firearm fatalities per capita; percent of children not living with father. We organized these thirteen strongest predictors of life expectancy in categories of wealth, human and social capital, safety, environment, and family, which inform the pivotal areas of power. Finally, we ranked the life expectancy of Black people in counties and metropolitan areas across the country, examining how they performed across the various constructs and exploring how communities are gaining power in specific locations.

The index helps us identify the social factors that most affect Black people's life expectancy and highlights areas that perform better or worse than expected. Similar to the way meteorologists use models to predict the weather, we use our model to predict life expectancy. In Fairfax County, Virginia, for example, the life expectancy for Black people predicted by the model is eighty-two years, but the county exceeded this by one year. In fact, many counties and metro areas across the country surpass national averages and our predictions, suggesting that civic action and power can have a significant impact on longevity.

Our model identified 55 percent of the causes for differences in Black life expectancy, focusing on those that are most important. While these are not the only predictors of longevity, they are the most statistically significant. Some structural factors, such as air pollution, are less controllable by individuals, whereas behaviors such as reducing gun fatalities are more within their control. Overall, our findings indicate that people in certain locales can influence elements that affect their life expectancy. In the area where I live, Prince George's County, Maryland, life expectancy is 77.5 (close to the model's prediction). A close look at Prince George's County allows us to see the circumstances and conditions that contribute to its residents' life expectancy and provides insights others might examine in their locale.

THE TOP 20 U.S. COUNTIES WITH THE HIGHEST BLACK PROGRESS INDEX SCORE, LIFE EXPECTANCY, AND LIFE YEARS UNEXPLAINED BY MODEL

County	State	Metropolitan Area	Black Progress Index	Life Expectancy at Birth	Unexplained Years of Life	Black Population, 2020
Putnam	New York	New York-Newark-Jersey City, NY-NJ-PA	83.5	85.8	2.3	3,349
Warrick	Indiana	Evansville, IN-KY	83.2	-	-	1,147
Scott	Minnesota	Minneapolis-St. Paul-Bloomington, MN-WI	82.9	89.7	6.8	6,286
Cumberland	Maine	Portland-South Portland, ME	82.8	79.7	-3.1	9,192
Loudon	Virginia	Washington-Arlington-Alexandria, DC-VA-MD-WV	82.7	82.4	-0.3	31,241
Collier	Florida	Naples-Marco Island, FL	82.6	86.0	3.4	25,613
Rockingham	New Hampshire	Boston-Cambridge-Newton, MA-NH	82.2	82.2	0.0	2,704
Fairfax	Virginia	Washington-Arlington-Alexandria, DC-VA-MD-WV	82.2	83.1	0.9	112,024
Snohomish	Washington	Seattle-Tacoma-Bellevue, WA	82.2	83.1	1.0	26,644
Delaware	Ohio	Columbus, OH	82.0	79.3	-2.7	7,153
Prince William	Virginia	Washington-Arlington-Alexandria, DC-VA-MD-WV	81.8	79.3	-2.5	97,848
Washington	Oregon	Portland-Vancouver-Hillsboro, OR-WA	81.6	82.5	1.0	12,931
Barnstable	Massachusetts	Barnstable Town, MA	81.5	76.5	-4.9	6,098
Wright	Minnesota	Minneapolis-St. Paul-Bloomington, MN-WI	81.4	82.8	1.4	2,366
Forsythe	Georgia	Atlanta-Sandy Springs-Alpharetta, GA	81.4	81.4	0.0	8,574
Saratoga	New York	Albany-Schenectady-Troy, NY	81.4	81.8	0.4	3,906
Montgomery	Maryland	Washington-Arlington-Alexandria, DC-VA-MD-WV	81.3	81.1	-0.2	193,450
Nassau	New York	New York-Newark-Jersey City, NY-NJ-PA	81.3	79.0	-2.3	157,724
Dallas	Iowa	Des Moines-West Des Moines, IA	81.2	85.8	4.7	1,720

* * *

Not surprisingly, some of the most important predictors of life expectancy involve wealth, narrowly defined as the total value of everything individuals and families own minus their debts. Possessions and financial prosperity grant people physical comfort and set their living standards.[4] Of the multitude of variables that come under the category of wealth, median household income, homeownership, and business ownership emerged as the most influential.

In Prince George's County, which is one of the wealthiest majority-Black locations in the United States, the median Black family income is approximately $87,000, which is in the 98th percentile, very high among all Black people in the United States. According to the 2020 US census, Prince George's County had a population of 967,201, making it the second-most populous county in the state, after Montgomery County. Given its proximity to the nation's federal district, Prince George's is home to several federal government facilities, including Joint Base Andrews and the United States Census Bureau's headquarters. It is this access to government employers that helps drive Prince George's wealth, which in turn drives higher life expectancy.

According to a 2016 study in the *Journal of the American Medical Association*, the disparity in life expectancy between the wealthiest and poorest 1 percent stood at 14.6 years for men and 10.1 years for women.[5] This gap had widened over time: between 2001 and 2014, the top 5 percent of income earners saw an increase of 2.34 years for men and 2.91 years for women, while those in the bottom

5 percent experienced much smaller gains—0.32 years for men and a mere 0.04 years for women.

The study also showed that life expectancy for individuals with lower incomes varied significantly by location. In the lowest income quartile, there was an approximately 4.5-year gap in life expectancy in different areas, suggesting that place matters. The increase in life expectancy from 2001 to 2014 also exhibited considerable variation according to location, ranging from gains of over four years to losses of more than two years. The researchers found that geographic disparities for those in the lowest income quartile were closely linked with health behaviors such as smoking, but not significantly associated with factors such as access to medical care, physical environment, income inequality, or labor market conditions. The researchers clearly delved into the ongoing debate of whether structural factors that are less in the control of residents, such as the level of access to medical care, or behaviors that are more within individuals' control, like smoking, are the primary cause of life expectancy differences. However, structural factors and behaviors are interrelated. Policies that privileged whiteness are foundational to the racial disparities that favor white people. Policies that sap resources and opportunity help produce worse outcomes, meaning behaviors. US policy has long had a tendency to blame Black people for poverty, rather than policy driven by anti-Black legislation, a tendency starkly on display in *The Negro Family: The Case for National Action*, the 1965 report authored by Daniel Patrick Moynihan.[6] Researchers share the tendency to subtly blame Black people as well.

Focusing on the downstream effects of policy, including

negative behaviors, can often be another backhanded way of blaming low-income Black people. Both everyday racism and racism across a lifetime are associated with incidences of obesity, for example.[7] For this reason, morbid obesity cannot be addressed through fat-shaming, but rather through reforming systems and adopting behavioral intervention strategies that include access to fresh foods, safe walkable areas, and dietitians.

The Black Progress Index shows, not surprisingly, that homeownership is another significant predictor of life expectancy. The higher the percentage of Black homeowners in a metro area or county, the higher the life expectancy. The positive connection between homeownership and health is intuitive: when people own their homes, they tend to have more stable living environments, reducing the stress of frequent relocation and housing insecurity. Owning a home fosters a sense of security, providing a strong foundation for physical and mental well-being.

But with a homeownership rate of only 41.7 percent, Black households have the lowest national share, 30 percentage points lower than that of white households, according to a 2023 report.[8] This is even higher in thirty-seven states, with gaps exceeding 40 percentage points in ten states. In Prince George's County, the Black homeownership rate is 61 percent, almost 20 points higher than the national average. Given America's centuries-old history of legal housing discrimination—from the legacies of slavery to Jim Crow segregation, redlining, and other anti-Black policies—we know that systemic racism plays a significant role in current homeownership rates.

Economist Casey Breen, who looked for causal factors

linking homeownership to life expectancy, confirmed this intuition.[9] Homeownership helps families accumulate wealth, which can provide a safety net in times of economic hardship. This financial security can translate to better access to health care, nutritious food, and recreational activities, all of which are crucial components of a longer, healthier life. Stability does indeed lead to lower levels of chronic stress, a known factor in health outcomes. Homeowners also often have a greater sense of control over their environment, which can lead to neighborhood changes, contributing to a higher quality of life. Homeowners typically have a vested interest in maintaining their properties and neighborhoods, which enhances stronger social connections and community engagement.

It is common to attribute low rates of Black homeownership to a lack of financial literacy, a woefully insufficient strategy to improve those rates and wealth outcomes. Rather, America's history of legal discrimination in housing is responsible for shaping the culture surrounding who gets to own property, as well as home-buying practices and products. Education on how housing markets work could certainly benefit all potential home buyers, especially those who have had limited opportunities to acquire real estate due to past and present de facto and de jure discrimination.

But it's not ignorance of markets that keeps people from purchasing a home so much as it is the lack of a down payment. The thinking that education predicts wealth is wrongheaded. Wealth predicts education—it's surprising how financially literate a group seems to become as its net worth grows—and a promissory note of financial literacy cannot make up for the lack of equity rooted in the absence of intergenerational wealth due to discrimination. Education is not a means to fill some kind of cultural deficiency, but it can provide the information people need to change the systems that can grant them access to life-extending assets. Also crucial is the wherewithal to demand mortgage products that acknowledge past discrimination and wealth inequality.

The positive effects of homeownership on life expectancy extend to business proprietorship. Black entrepreneurship plays a relatively modest yet meaningful role in predicting longevity. Approximately 1 percent of Black adults between the ages of eighteen and sixty-four are owners of employer businesses, and a one-standard-deviation increase in ownership rates corresponds to an estimated increase of about 0.2 years in life expectancy. Notably, in Hidalgo County, Texas, the Black business ownership rate reaches as high as 4 percent, coinciding with a Black life expectancy of 91.5 years. The Black business ownership rate in Prince George's County is 0.6, which places it in the 93rd percentile.

Of the thirteen different index components, being born outside the United States has the largest effect on Black life expectancy. The greater number of Black immigrants residing in a county or metro area, the higher the average rate of life expectancy is in that area. One standard deviation in this variable in a county adds one year to the predicted life expectancy for Black people living there. The causal reason is unclear; it may be a pure composition effect, in that foreign-born Black Americans enjoy better health than the native Black population. Black immigrants born outside the United States do tend to live longer than those born in the country, with a notable gap of eight years for women and ten years for men. This difference persists even among Black adults covered by Medicare, suggesting that access to health insurance doesn't account for it. Other possibilities are that foreign-born Black Americans tend to reside in or move to counties that offer other health-related advantages.

In Cass County, North Dakota, in the Fargo metro area, 73 percent of the Black population is foreign-born, and Black life expectancy reaches 78.6. In another example, Scott County, Minnesota, in the Minneapolis metro area, 63 percent of the Black population is foreign-born—still a high percentage—and life expectancy reaches 89.7 years.

There is an enduring debate between descendants of American slaves and African and Caribbean Americans on the degree to which culture and attitudes, rather than structural racism, shape different outcomes for such factors of longevity as health and education. Perceptions of Africans and Caribbean Americans somewhat reflect the myth of the Asian American model minority: their culture makes them smart, hardworking, thrifty, and entrepreneurial. Sociologist John Ogbu, who explored frameworks for understanding disparities in school performance among minority groups, distinguished between voluntary and involuntary minorities. Voluntary minorities are groups that migrated to a new society by choice; involuntary minorities were brought to that society through processes such as slavery or colonization. Ogbu argued that these distinct historical experiences shape these groups' cultural and psychological orientations, influencing their educational outcomes.

The same is true of health. Research on the differences

between immigrants and their second- and third-generation family members provide compelling evidence for the persistence of structural racism. Foreign-born Black Americans show generational changes when self-reporting overall health, with third-generation Americans noting poor health at much higher rates than first-generation immigrants. A 2020 study shows that the rate of intergenerational health dissipation may be increasing, as the second generation reports lower health than nonimmigrant youth, especially if they are in a lower socioeconomic bracket.[10] The positive benefits of immigration status seem to dissipate with every passing generation, suggesting that American racism is bad for your health.

Education is also a significant contributor to better health. Although Americans are instilled with the idea that diligent effort in school and high academic achievement can lead to a middle-class lifestyle, data shows that a good education cannot close wealth gaps. However, educated communities do correlate with better health outcomes. The individual effect of education on health is well established. Empirical evidence from hundreds of studies has shown a clear "gradient," indicating that higher levels of education are associated with better health and longer life.[11] Education influences access to information, income, safe neighborhoods, and healthier lifestyles, all of which contribute to better health. Likewise, less or low-quality education restricts access to the material and immaterial goods that enhance longevity. Also, living near higher-income adults may also boost health by improving access to nutritious food, exercise, safety, good jobs, and other life-enhancing resources.[12] The Black Progress Index shows that the percentage of adults aged twenty-five and over with at least a bachelor's degree adds 0.38 years for every standard deviation.

Prince George's County shows high performance in most influential factors in the index but underperforms in K–12 schooling. Nineteen percent of its public-school students score at or above proficiency in math, which places the county in the 12th percentile. It is this gap that contributes to the county's relatively low life expectancy, since Prince George's counts Black residents who have a bachelor's degree or higher at 35 percent, which places it in the 94th percentile. This is because many highly educated Black people move to the region or study in one of the many universities in the area. High college attainment correlates with greater life expectancy in other urban areas.

The rate of college attainment is high in the Atlanta, Baltimore, and Washington, DC, metro areas, including Forsyth County, Georgia (56 percent); Howard County, Maryland (54 percent); and Arlington and Loudoun counties, Virginia (51 percent and 50 percent, respectively). Life expectancy for Black adults in these places is similarly high, ranging from 79.4 in Howard County to 82.4 in Loudoun County. At the opposite end, the Black college attainment rate is just 4.4 in Baker County, Florida, outside of Jacksonville, and life expectancy there is 76.4. Butts County, Georgia, outside of Atlanta, has the same low college attainment rate and even lower life expectancy, at 73.8.

Another explanation of the beneficial effects of education on health is that health knowledge as well as access to information can make a positive impact. People with higher levels of education, numeracy, and literacy are found both to exhibit higher levels of health knowledge and to engage in healthier behaviors. Diverse social networks—which predict better health—may also increase health knowledge by providing greater access to what works.

The Black Progress Index found that the greater the spatial distance of Facebook friends, the higher the positive correlation to longer life. Distance in one's social network is associated with higher education and economic mobility, which, as we know, are key contributors to better health. In the 2020 Brookings report "How Social Networks Impact Economic Mobility," Camille Busette and her coauthors emphasize, "The significance of social networks cannot be overstated. They offer access to crucial elements like support, information, influence, and resources, which are often overlooked in discussions of opportunity structures. Social capital is a key factor in determining mobility."[13]

The mean distance of Facebook friends in Prince George's County is 648 miles, which places the county in the 85th percentile. Comparably, the mean distance of Facebook friends in Jackson, Mississippi, which has a life expectancy of 72.6 years, is 193 miles, which places it in the 8th percentile.

* * *

ONE SURPRISING FINDING is that there is a negative correlation between rates of religious membership and Black longevity. People living in areas where there is greater religious affiliation have lower life expectancies, although the same people usually self-report better health. There could be some composition effects with churchgoers, such as a greater likelihood of being obese.[14] Praying for Jesus "to take the wheel" might result in poorer outcomes, leading to a lack of agency when dealing with health issues. Regions with higher levels of religious involvement may also exhibit other factors detrimental to health, such as increased crime rates, limited access to nutritious food, and higher levels of pollution.

Another factor in the correlation between religious affiliation and lower life expectancy could be communal stress. Churchgoers are often targets of discrimination who have experienced trauma and are unhealthy because of it. Public health researcher Anita Chandra and her colleagues have expanded the medical concept of allostatic load—that is, the cumulative effect of chronic stress on an individual—applying the concept to entire communities. They found that community environment significantly affects individual allostatic load, with evidence indicating that health disparities arise from exposure to physical, social, and psychosocial stressors. Also, persistent stress, with its negative impact on individuals, has bearing on their social networks, communal structures, and membership organizations. The extent of religious membership could reflect stress and trauma at the community level.

When it comes to church membership, Prince George's County is in the 40th percentile, which is relatively low compared to a place like Jackson, Mississippi, which is in the 89th percentile. Accordingly, residents of Prince George's live on average five years longer than those in Jackson.

* * *

BLACK POWER MOVEMENTS of the past have consistently made community safety a goal, and this, too, has bearing on life expectancy: low levels of gun violence and homicides correlate with high rates of people commuting to work by bicycle or walking. Low levels of gun violence would seem to inculcate greater comfort in movement. Having the ability to walk to your job, school, or other basic, day-to-day destinations—the so-called fifteen-minute neighborhood—offers opportunities for passive exercise, which is associated with lower rates of obesity.

Prince George's County is a relatively safe place, in the 12th percentile for gun fatalities. The impact of gun violence on community safety is straightforward, severely reducing years of expected life while also creating intense levels of fear, grief, and uncertainty for those directly affected and for those proximate to it. Neighborhood gun violence affects life expectancies in other ways, by deepening poverty and health inequity and by projecting assumptions about the unworthiness of communities for various forms of investment. Although the number of perpetrators of gun violence is small in relation to a location's overall population, negative perceptions extend to entire areas as a kind of collateral damage. They then serve to justify withholding investment in or divesting from Black neighborhoods, exacerbating the structural disadvantages already existing within these communities.

Other safety-predicting variables that are related to high levels of discrimination—such as the number of police officers per capita, deaths from police encounters, hate crimes, and anti-Black hate crimes—were not statistically significant for Black life expectancy, unlike gun violence. Thus, policies and programs that address root causes of gun violence are essential to promoting safety and power.

* * *

LONGEVITY IS ALSO correlated with family composition. In the average county, 57 percent of Black children do not live with their fathers, according to Census Bureau data. This matters for several reasons, but one is straightforward: when they live in the same household, Black fathers invest heavily in their children in terms of play, reading, helping with homework, and other activities. Those who don't live in the same household spend much less time on these activities.[15] A father's involvement, in turn, predicts healthier behavior from their children, such as reduced rates of smoking.[16] In Prince George's County, 42 percent of children don't live with their fathers, which places it in the 18th percentile. Controlling for their living arrangements, Black fathers spend at least as much time as non-Hispanic white fathers do engaging with their children. CDC data shows that Black fathers who live with their children have the same if not higher rates of involvement as other racial groups.[17] A Pew Research Center study found that of fathers who don't live with their children, Black men (67 percent) are most likely to see their children monthly or more (compared to 59 percent of white fathers and 32 percent of Hispanic fathers).[18] However, Black fathers are more than twice as likely to live apart from their children as non-Hispanic white men, so the overall effect is less-than-average involvement.

Many factors affect the probability of paternal involvement, including the degree of parental conflict, quality of past family relationships, and whether the father has ever been incarcerated.[19] A 2006 study that examined the associations between family conflict and the quality of boys' friendships in divorced and nondivorced families found that marital conflict was associated with low levels of reasoning in mother-son and sibling-brother relationships in nondivorced families, and with low levels of reasoning in father-son relationships in divorced families. Family conflict-resolution strategies that helped to mediate the connections between marital conflict and boys' friendships with their peers improved their quality. Thus a focus on conflict resolution seemingly can bear fruit in marital as well as nonmarital relationships involving children and can ultimately enhance Black power relationship building.

*   *   *

PREDICTABLY, ENVIRONMENTAL QUALITY, measured by low levels of air pollution and living in moderate- or low-population-density areas, correlates with longer life. Among the many types of pollutants, air pollution ranks as one of the most potent drags on life expectancy. According to a 2022 report by the Energy Policy Institute at the University of Chicago, air pollution, which is mostly caused by burning fossil fuels, takes 2.2 years off the average global life expectancy.[20] Compounding matters, the legacies of racist infrastructure policies have marooned some Black-majority communities in low-lying areas at heightened risk of flooding or in concrete-heavy urban environments with less green space to help lower the temperatures and reduce the impact of heat waves.[21] Because of the latter, many Black people swelter through temperatures two degrees hotter on average and six to eight degrees hotter in more extreme locations.[22]

The negative effect of population density on life

expectancy is somewhat surprising. Density is typically associated with increased economic productivity due to easier access to markets, labor, resources, innovation and creativity, and robust social networks. However, less-dense places performed better on the Black Progress Index, possibly due to the compensatory advantage of small to mid-size cities. It is worth noting that Prince George's, with its higher-than-average life expectancy, is a very dense place, ranking in the 94th percentile.

We find that population density is only weakly correlated with air pollution, but it is very strongly correlated with intensity of land use and lack of tree cover. Low-population-density areas do not necessarily have cleaner air or water—but they are exposed to more natural environments, including trees. Beyond the focus on life expectancy, this research is relevant to quality of life more broadly. Drawing on large sample microdata from Gallup and Sharecare, it transpires that, not surprisingly, Black people evaluate their lives more positively in counties with higher life expectancy.

* * *

FROM AN AFRO-PESSIMIST perspective, American society is dependent upon racism and anti-Black violence for its proper functioning, whereby Black suffering is an instrument for societal growth. This theory comes to life in the public square when intellectuals are asked whether they have hope for the future. While ideas of Afro-pessimism mostly reverberate within academic circles, research on racial disparities that restricts itself to national comparisons often masks evidence of racial progress that could offer reasons for optimism.

The fact of progress and stagnation in Black life expectancy in different locations makes clear that people have some agency. When we take an overly optimistic or pessimistic view of the state of Black America and treat it as a monolith, we ignore localized stories of growth, determination, and thriving. The diversity of places where Black people are living longer and thriving suggests that it is due to some extent to the people themselves. In these places, individuals, civil rights groups, organizers, and politicians are helping to dismantle the architecture of inequality that takes away years of life. There is reason for optimism. Black power is present, and we see it at the local level. We should look to those locales for solutions.

3

FORTY ACRES
AND A MALL

As the Civil War drew to a close, two years after President Abraham Lincoln issued the Emancipation Proclamation, Union general William T. Sherman convened a meeting on January 12, 1865, with Secretary of War Edwin M. Stanton and twenty Black ministers to address the urgent issue of safeguarding and providing for the numerous Black refugees who had trailed Sherman's army since his invasion of Georgia nearly two months prior. Shaping the agenda, a primary question was posed to the ministers: "What do you want for your own people?"[1]

The Black ministers had designated the sixty-seven-year-old Reverend Garrison Frazier as their spokesperson. Frazier, who had acquired his and his wife's freedom eight years earlier by paying $1,000 in gold and silver, was asked what he understood about the Emancipation Proclamation. He responded, "The freedom as I understand it, promised by the proclamation, is taking us from under the yoke of bondage, and placing us where we could reap the fruit of our own labor, take care of ourselves, and assist the Government in maintaining our freedom."[2]

As for what the leaders wanted for Black people, Frazier added, "The way we can best take care of ourselves is to have land, and turn it and till it by our own labor—that is, by the labor of the women and children and old men; and we can soon maintain ourselves and have something to spare."

Frazier's statement is recognized as the first call for reparations, a system of redress for egregious injustices. Those charged with ending the war shared an interest in Frazier's pragmatic goals of self-determination and self-sufficiency. Abolitionists Charles Sumner, Thaddeus Stevens, and other Republicans had fervently pushed for land redistribution as a political means to dismantle the power of southern slaveholders. General Sherman was certainly no friend of Black people or abolitionists, but he did desire to punish Confederates who refused to yield to the rule of law.

Four days after this meeting, on January 16, Sherman issued Special Field Order No. 15. This directive claimed a stretch of coastline from Charleston, South Carolina, to the St. Johns River in Florida as Union property. Approximately four hundred thousand acres of this land were allocated to newly emancipated Americans in parcels of forty acres each, marking a redistribution initiative. Additionally, some families were to receive mules no longer needed for the war; hence the notion of forty acres and a mule.[3] But after Lincoln's assassination on April 14, 1865, the directive was reversed, and the land allocated to Black families was returned to white Confederate landowners.

Since General Sherman's signing of Field Order 15,

Black people have insistently pursued land and business ownership in their quest for self-determination. Being able to own and operate an enterprise in property or land that you also own is a key measure of Black power.

As we know, Black people represent 14 percent of the population but only 2.7 percent of employer firms, that is, businesses with more than one employee. Increasing the share of employer firms to match the Black population would yield more than six hundred thousand businesses. However, that goal would be easier to reach if Black people owned more real estate to house those firms—"to have land, and turn it and till it by our own labor." Owning commercial real estate would help combat the racial wealth gap that underlies lack of ownership in other areas. The alternative, which is to rent property, exacerbates the wealth gap. Tenants bear the brunt of economic shocks, which are reflected in abrupt hikes in rent and sudden changes in ownership.

My colleagues Jonathan Rothwell and Tracy Loh and I found that 81 percent of nonresidential commercial property, which includes retail shops, offices, and waterfront warehouses, is owned by the top 1 percent of earners.[4] Only 3 percent of Black earners own nonresidential commercial real estate, compared to 8 percent of white earners. For those that do own commercial property, the average white earner holds it to the value of $34,000, compared to just $3,600 for the average Black earner. Ownership of these income-generating assets is extraordinarily concentrated in the hands of a few. Increasing the percentage of Black people who own commercial real estate, among all socio-economic classes, represents a significant Black power goal.

* * *

ORIOLE PARK AT Camden Yards in Baltimore was built to provide baseball fans with more than just enjoyment of the sport. Nestled ten minutes west of the Inner Harbor, the facility blends in with the charmingly developed section of downtown. At the game, spectators don't feel as if they are inside a stadium—they experience the game as a friendly part of a neighborhood. On a hot summer's day at the ballpark, it's a pleasure to walk down the block to enjoy a sweet frozen mango dessert to cool down and pass the time. There are vendors throughout Camden Yards—budding entrepreneurs offering a fresh slice of Americana.

Oriole Park is the kind of development that cities long for. The 7th Inning Sorbet stands there evoke images of young, hardworking entrepreneurs operating a small neighborhood business out of a Main Street storefront. Made with fresh fruit, the sorbets are low in sugar and nondairy, a welcome alternative to the traditional peanuts and Cracker Jacks offered during baseball games. Frozen Desert Sorbet & Café, the parent company of 7th Inning Sorbet, is more than a business. It's part of Rasheed Aziz's effort to develop both people and place.

Aziz leads Citywide Youth Development, a nonprofit organization that "uses manufacturing and entrepreneurship to elevate a new economic framework for youth and young adults," according to its website.[5] Participants are involved in two distinct entrepreneurial programs: Frozen Desert Sorbet & Café and Made in B'more apparel. The Frozen Desert Sorbet & Café offers a variety of products, including all-natural fruit-based sorbet, salads, pizza, smoothies, and more. Made in B'more specializes in urban "athleisure," such as jackets, hoodies, hats, and other clothing, all produced within the ten-thousand-square-foot Entrepreneurs Making and Growing Enterprises (EMAGE) Center, which is located in West Baltimore, 3.5 miles and a world away from Camden Yards. Supported by a state bond, grants from Baltimore City government, and philanthropic organizations as well as private donations, the EMAGE Center opened in 2021 during the pandemic. Revenues generated from its companies as well as state and city development dollars, philanthropic giving, and individual contributions sustain its operations.

When someone says "West Baltimore," wholesome entrepreneurialism and charming neighborhoods don't typically come to mind. Instead, what surfaces are images of poverty, blight, death, drugs, police, and Black people. The EMAGE Center represents Aziz's mission to change the negative perceptions—and especially outcomes—of Black men in the city and the built environment—that is, the man-made conditions, including the commercial and residential properties, of their lives. Whether negative ideas of Baltimore emanated from *The Wire*, from the fires and rioting in the aftermath of Freddie Gray's murder by police in 2015, or from the lived experiences of its residents, the circumstances in which the community lives have become indivisible from the people themselves.

According to the Black Progress Index, Black life expectancy in Baltimore falls slightly below seventy years. However, a mere forty-five-minute drive south along I-95, in Prince George's and Montgomery counties, Black individuals live notably longer—another eight to thirteen years, respectively. Black homeownership in the city stands at 43 percent, positioning it in the 42nd percentile, and just 12 percent of its public-school students demonstrate proficiency in math. The rate of Black firearm fatalities places the city in the 99th percentile, and a staggering 62 percent of Black children do not reside with their fathers. Roughly fifteen thousand properties, or between 7 percent and 8 percent of the city's housing stock, are unoccupied, according to a 2022 Johns Hopkins study.

Aziz is right to approach the development of people and place simultaneously. A central premise of this book is that transformation and growth come when we invest in the people *and* the settings in which they live. The participants in Citywide Youth Development don't live in a ballpark, but they deserve similar investment. But given the range of issues that determine longevity and well-being, there is always the question of where to start. I take the position that we should prioritize investment in the strongest assets of residents, which will help meet their other pressing needs.

Despite its numerous challenges, Baltimore places highly when it comes to Black business ownership, ranking in the 84th percentile. However, most of the Black-owned businesses in the city's metro area are sole proprietorships. There are 2,331 Black-owned businesses with employees, which make up just 4.5 percent of all businesses in the metropolitan area. If the number of Black-owned businesses matched the city's Black population of 31.3 percent, there would be a total of 22,862 Black-owned businesses. This means 20,531 more businesses would be added to reach that 31.3 percent share. The growth would transform local and regional economies. Black businesses create an average of seven jobs per firm, compared to twenty-two for all businesses. If the average employees reached parity, there would be approximately 33,254 new jobs. But if the number of Black businesses matched the population size and the employees per firm matched the average business, there would be 479,848 jobs.

However, the potential growth of these businesses is undermined by the negative perceptions of majority-Black neighborhoods, which are littered with vacant and dilapidated lots that Black people don't own or have the power to refurbish. If we can better understand how unwarranted, negative perceptions influence public and private investment, we can begin to see that the neighborhoods of West Baltimore are worthy of development dollars. To look at the perceptions of businesses in Black neighborhoods, my colleague Jonathan Rothwell and I examined the financial performance and customer ratings of private enterprises in cities throughout the country, comparing levels of quality across racial groups and neighborhoods.[6] As Black elders used to say, "Our ice is just as cold." It turns out the saying holds up empirically. Among other important findings, we saw that Black-, Latino-, and Asian-owned companies score just as high on Yelp as their white peers. Many Black businesses are underappreciated assets that could be scaled with investment. The problem is that revenue does not follow quality.

Our business study found that in mostly white neighborhoods, revenue from businesses with high Yelp ratings was 8.5 percent to 9 percent higher. Poorly rated businesses in these areas grew much less, between 5 percent and 7.5 percent. However, in neighborhoods where most residents are Black, both highly and poorly rated business revenue only grew by about 7 percent, which is even less than the growth of poorly rated businesses in areas with very few Black residents. We also found that Yelp scores decline as the Black population in proximity to the business increases. But the negative perceptions of the merits of Black businesses often aren't warranted. The declining scores are instead driven by customers being less likely to frequent quality businesses in Black neighborhoods, a dynamic that hurts both consumers and business owners. In addition, highly rated businesses that are devalued are effectively forced to compete with low-rated businesses. Ideally, high-performing businesses should stand out and reap the rewards of higher quality. We estimate that negative perceptions cost high-quality businesses upward of $4 billion annually. Worse, a biased market cuts at the heart of opportunity by negating the hard work, agency, and self-determination of business owners.

In Baltimore, proprietors are forced to contend with high vacancy rates, which certainly do not help bring them the customers they deserve. Baltimore's vacancies invite blight and criminal activity, deter foot traffic, decrease property values, reduce local revenues, and create neighborhood ugliness. None of these are conducive to business growth, let alone human development. While some blame residents for neighborhood conditions, renters have only limited responsibility for buildings they don't own. The owners responsible for vacant or poorly maintained properties often do not reside anywhere near their buildings. Cities have limited resources and systems to hold landlords accountable for neglect of their buildings. Also, a lack of municipal maintenance in the form of cracked and uneven sidewalks, potholes and damaged road surfaces, overgrown landscaping, and broken streetlights adds insult to injury. Unrealized tax revenues do not help matters. There is a clear problem to be solved. City leaders want responsible property owners, and Black people, especially entrepreneurs, want and need more real estate and responsive governments. The inventory to meet these needs is often lying vacant in plain sight, but there is no framework for converting residents into property owners. Existing businesses could be scaled to generate the kind of wealth and job opportunities that can transform and sustain entire neighborhoods, but they need to operate in conditions that are conducive for growth. Struggling, half-vacant commercial corridors present a reasonable solution: an opportunity to foster multiple property and business owners in one place.

Many current initiatives related to business expansion, purchasing commercial real estate, and improving neighborhoods are typically managed by city or state community and economic development departments. These related sectors originate from distinct policy histories and practices, but economic development and community development both broadly entail planned investments that lead to neighborhood improvement and regional economic growth, resulting in residents' increased wealth, opportunity, and well-being. All such development projects require private investment capital, but investors don't put their money into things unless they expect economic and social returns. However, Black homes, businesses, and commercial real estate—among other assets—tend to be undervalued, having much greater worth than the level at which they are priced. Similar to our analyses of residential property, Jonathan Rothwell, Tracy Loh, and I found that commercial real estate is valued differently depending on the Black share of population living in the area. We found that in majority-Black zip codes, devaluation results in aggregate wealth losses of $171 billion for retail real estate.

One of the most pernicious aspects of devaluation based on race is that investors don't see the worth they would see if those same assets were in white neighborhoods. Rather, based on negative assumptions, they manufacture a layer of risk, which is shouldered by Black people and communities. That racialized risk increases the cost of capital and the cost of community and economic development—a form of "Black tax." In fact, these neighborhoods have underappreciated assets that would grow with investment. Consequently, Black communities need an equity-driven capital stack—different types of capital, including private, governmental, and philanthropic sources—that minimizes or negates the risk assumed by racism and helps residents purchase property and scale businesses.

Further, community development strategies that seek to build one entrepreneur or storefront at a time, as most initiatives do, won't significantly alter the status quo, given the scale of racial wealth and ownership divides. Only larger community development projects can create impact. Conversely, development projects that are too large in scale are an economic shock to a community, raising the cost of living beyond the capacity of long-term residents. Ideally, development should be designed so that community members have a share in their own growth.

Authentic community development strikes a balance between investing in people and investing in places, going beyond brick and mortar. Jobs with higher incomes and tax incentives help residents keep pace with the inevitable cost-of-living increase that comes with economic development. Shared or collective ownership opportunities not only accomplish these goals; they can also change the current ownership structures that benefit the few. A collective development approach that empowers people and places simultaneously is needed to make community development live up to its name.

* * *

THROUGH HIS REAL estate company, Chicago TREND, Lyneir Richardson is revitalizing dormant shopping centers and strip malls in communities of color, turning them into hubs for entrepreneurial activity and growth. Purchasing depreciating assets isn't a new business model—it's been a central feature of gentrification across the country. Wealthy for-profit companies and private developers regularly take advantage of the lower prices of property in Black neighborhoods to acquire and develop areas in ways that create more renters than owners. Investments from the development raise the value of the property, but because local residents aren't owners, they don't reap the profits. They also often can't keep pace with the rising cost of living in the area and are priced out.

TREND's mission goes beyond typical property acquisition and storefront leasing; its goal is to create opportunities for local communities to invest in these projects, in their neighborhoods, and ultimately in themselves. What's novel about Richardson's approach is that he extends an invitation for community members to become stakeholders, co-owners with the developer through a crowd-sourcing platform, which allows for smaller dollar investments. Community members then have an equity stake in the financing that also includes debt capital, tax credits, philanthropic giving, and the private investments Richardson receives. Normally, to be an accredited investor, a person or firm must have sizable wealth to qualify and participate. New crowd-sourcing platforms allow for individual residents to put up as little as $1,000 to have an equity stake in the development. In addition, Richardson's focus on strip malls breathes life into often abandoned or dilapidated assets that are at the heart of many predominately Black neighborhoods.

Like many, Richardson was moved by the murder of George Floyd by four Minneapolis police officers while he was in their custody on Memorial Day in 2020. Video footage of the killing came to symbolize the repression, control, and disregard of Black people and their communities. The massive international protests that followed prompted corporations—including Apple, Bank of America, Comcast, Nike, and dozens more—to invest billions in fighting racism and inequality.[7] During the protests, Richardson saw a middle-aged Black man like himself hold up a sign in front of a shopping center, pleading. "Don't wreck this building," the sign said. "Don't wreck this store; it's black-owned."

This plea, echoed by makeshift signs on storefronts nationwide, reflected real fear that looters might exploit the reduced law enforcement presence during the protests. Proprietors posting "spare my Black business" signs knew too well that looters aren't likely to consider the owner's race when targeting a store. "Our ice is just as cold" holds for theft, too. The underlying assumption and message of the posters was made clear by the act itself: communities tend to safeguard and care for assets when they have a stake in them.

This was the moment when Richardson realized he needed to change the nature of his work. Trained as a banking lawyer, he'd gotten a taste of development in his early twenties, through his involvement in loan contracts typically made between the bank and large publicly traded companies. He gained experience working on real estate deals worth hundreds of millions of dollars. But it wasn't until he took on a pro bono assignment that he began his immersion in retail and community development. "The bank gave the opportunity to handle a $100,000 loan to a Black man working to buy his building two miles away from a majority-Black neighborhood where I grew up in Chicago," he told me in an interview.

"I couldn't articulate it this way in my twenties. But getting resources to people and places that other people overlook or undervalue became my life's work." In his thirties, Richardson opened his own real estate development firm, using the profits from buying and selling properties and raising equity capital through philanthropic foundations. He primarily focused on low-income housing projects, which involved investing his own and other private investments, low-income housing tax credits (LIHTC), debt financing in the form of loans from banks or financial institutions, and grants and subsidies from government agencies and philanthropic organizations. He developed some three hundred single-family houses and townhomes, primarily in Black-majority areas. Eventually he sold the firm, admittedly to avoid a fire sale, and joined the second-largest owner, developer, and manager of shopping centers in Chicago. That's when Richardson began focusing on commercial real estate and retail, and after concentrating on shopping center deals for years he opened Chicago TREND in 2016.

Prior to the 2020 protests, Chicago TREND had primarily advised philanthropic organizations on where and how to increase property ownership among residents predominately in neighborhoods of color. After the events of 2020, Richardson felt compelled to rethink his focus. He confronted the reality that few commercial buildings are owned by Black community members, whose pride, presence, and patronage ultimately protect those properties. His work in cities had given him a front-row seat to the economic disadvantages of Black and Brown communities with low wealth, who live near commercial corridors, when it comes to acquiring property. "So, if my business is going to help close the racial wealth gap," he realized, "we are going to have to do ownership differently."

Developers don't often come up in conversations about racial justice. The word *developer* garners the same side-eye from Black residents as *insurance man* and *police officer*. Deservedly or not, it has become synonymous with *gentrifier* and *urban planner*, those who create projects that price out residents. But real estate developers, the professionals who purchase land and finance deals, are pivotal actors in the building of housing, retail space, transportation hubs, and other projects that are critical to economic mobility and well-being.

Of course there should be development without displacement. "Economic and community development" implies that people should be able to stay in neighborhoods long enough to grow. Too often, though, Black residents are not even an afterthought in development projects. Even worse, "growth" is presumed to occur when Black people are forced out of their communities. Ignoring Black people in urban planning is easy to do when none of them are in the room. In a 2023 study on the demographics of real estate developers, researchers Peter Eberhardt and Howard Wial found that Black and Hispanic people together make up less than 1 percent of the industry.[8] They estimated that if Black and Latino developers were proportionately represented, there would be more than twenty-three thousand Black and thirty-one thousand Hispanic people joining the industry, generating more than $106 billion in new revenue each year.

As in any field, diversity matters. Brown skin doesn't give anyone special professional powers or better ethics, but it does offer insights. Developers who grew up in Black- and Latino-majority neighborhoods are more likely to recognize and value those lives and property, and at least see them as worthy of investment. Consequently, the effort to acquire commercial real estate should coincide with a plan to increase the number of Black developers who manage large-scale projects.

All real estate developers aim to buy land and develop property to sell the assets at a profit. They require capital—either equity or debt—to acquire properties and execute the necessary work, which places most Black people, who have fewer resources and less wealth, at a disadvantage. It took Richardson thirty years to cultivate the up-front capital from the profits accrued through buying and selling property to be able to purchase shopping malls. He now has five in major markets across the country.

From the moment a commercial property is acquired until the development's tenants begin offering services and paying rent, a span of twelve to twenty-four months can pass without the investment generating revenue. Navigating municipal processes and zoning regulations, negotiating loan agreements, securing credit approval, and construction time and costs all contribute to the overall expenses and duration of the project. Some developers purchase property with "slow" or "patient" capital, with limited expectation of turning a quick profit, but most are unwilling to sacrifice immediate returns for a larger future payback. Troubled communities rarely have the privilege of slow capital, and developers, regardless of race, tend to build projects that need high-income residents or tenants to meet growth projections. This leads to increased costs of living for people who may ultimately be priced out in a relatively short period of time. Richardson did not want to fall into that trap.

Having provided investment guidance to philanthropic organizations for years, Richardson believed he could support TREND's mission through grants available to nonprofit entities but not for-profit companies, enabling him to receive more patient forms of capital. So Richardson established TREND CDC as an in-house nonprofit partner. "Eighty percent of my up-front capital has been raised either from large philanthropic organizations or philanthropically motivated impact investors," said Richardson, empowering him to do the kind of community development that holds and uplifts residents instead of rejecting them.

So TREND looks for strip malls in Black-majority neighborhoods it believes are undervalued. "We do the due diligence and financial analysis to understand the conditions of the properties," said Richardson. "Often these are shopping centers that have been around for ten to seventy years. Some were around in many instances when the neighborhood was not majority Black." Richardson and TREND identified the West Baltimore strip mall, Edmondson Village Shopping Center, as an ideal place to do this work.

Located in West Baltimore, Edmondson Village Shopping Center was built by Joseph and Jacob Meyerhoff in 1947. It soon became a hot spot for retail for the entire city. Inspired by the architecture of Colonial Williamsburg, the shopping center was one of the first retail outlets designed for customers to reach by car. Anchored by a Hochschild, Kohn & Co. department store, Edmondson Village hosted nineteen different retailers. The strip mall also featured a bowling alley, drugstore, movie theater, and several acres of free parking, making it as much a social hub as a shopping destination. Many people remember the live monkeys that were displayed in the window of Hess Shoe Store as well as the Christmas lights festival that offered children a glimpse of Santa Claus. Black and white customers alike frequented Edmondson Village Shopping Center and reflect on it with great fondness.

Resident Lashelle Bynum said in a video, "Everything

was in this area for the families who lived here."[9] Bynum shared how she had viewed her first horror film at the movie theater. She had dined at the restaurants and shopped in the center's many stores. "We didn't go to downtown. . . . We didn't go to Westview. Everything was right here." She added, "It was such a beautiful place."

But the Meyerhoffs had constructed the shopping center during a period marked by transition.[10] The neighborhood underwent "white flight" when white residents moved westward to the suburbs. The construction of new highways contributed to the area's shift from a predominantly white population to a majority-Black one. Interestingly, the Meyerhoffs furthered this change by creating competition for themselves, establishing another shopping center west of the city in Catonsville. Throughout the eighties and nineties, occupancy in Edmondson Village Shopping Center dropped by as much as 50 percent. Many of the stores were replaced with more predatory businesses: check cashing and furniture rental outlets. By the aughts, the retail outlet mirrored the divestment and social decline being experienced in many Black neighborhoods in the city.

In 2019, a fire ravaged the center, resulting in the collapse of the roof over several stores.[11] Approximately ten businesses suffered damage. And in January 2023 it was the site of a mass shooting in which five young people were injured and one killed, the victims all students at Edmondson-Westside High School, which is across the street.[12] The once pride of Edmondson Village had become an eyesore and a drag on the neighborhood. However, Richardson saw the strip mall's potential.

Richardson took advantage of a series of modifications

to US Securities and Exchange Commission regulations through the American JOBS (Jumpstart Our Business Startups) Act, which permitted developers to use crowdfunding to raise capital from nonaccredited and accredited investors. Developers have often resorted to crowdfunding due to difficulties obtaining venture capital or loans from banks, but Richardson utilizes the SmallChange.co platform to democratize ownership.[13] Just as families pool funds for emergencies or to go on vacation, Richardson saw that communities can do the same to purchase property.

Over a period of three months, Richardson and his team canvassed residents of Edmondson Village and patrons of its shopping center, asking them whether they would like to participate in transforming the place. Word spread. Neighbors talked. Local media outlets covered the effort. "When is the last time anyone ever knocked on your door and intentionally invited you to be a co-owner of a development project?" Richardson asked. His actions stood in stark contrast to the developers who go door to door seeking to purchase property from vulnerable owners struggling to keep pace with the cost of living.

In the process of acquiring the site and garnering community investors, Richardson also worked to collect signatures to amend certain parts of a restrictive 1945 covenant related to Edmondson Avenue, including restrictions on multiuse residential buildings, architectural design, signage, and setback limitations.[14] There was also a campaign to eliminate a section of the covenant that, although unenforceable, barred occupation of the land specifically by "any Negro or person of Negro extraction" unless they were there as a servant.

In many ways, Baltimore's government had written the playbook for throttling property ownership and business growth.[15] In 1910, a Black Yale Law School graduate acquired a home in a formerly all-white neighborhood. The response from Baltimore's city government under the mayor at the time, J. Barry Mahool, was swift and stark: it introduced a residential segregation ordinance, confining African Americans to specific blocks. The mayor articulated the rationale behind this policy, stating that it was essential to isolate Black communities to mitigate civil unrest, prevent the spread of disease into neighboring white areas, and safeguard the property values of the white majority. This marked the commencement of a century-long era of federal, state, and local policies designed to confine Black people to slum areas.

In August 2023, Chicago TREND acquired Edmondson Village Shopping Center for $17 million, which included an investment of $3 million of its own money, $7.5 million from Baltimore City, $2 million from the state of Maryland, and $454,000 from two hundred community investors. Although the community share amounts to less than 3 percent of the deal, residents have a formal stake in the growth and direction of the mall, potentially enabling them to reap financial and social returns.

"We had the capital to complete the purchase with or without the community investors," Richardson said. "But the strategy was to knock on doors, to have meetings in church basements, apartment building common areas, and PTA meetings" so that residents would have skin in the game. Of the two hundred Black local small-dollar shareholders, the average investment was $2,275. Richardson dreams of bringing in a thousand community investors who each put in $2,000 or more. "They'll patronize, protect, and respect the shopping center in a way that will allow it to be more profitable and ultimately strengthen the neighborhood."

Richardson's project of buying strip malls and democratizing their ownership embodies Garrison Frazier's vision in 1865 "to have land, and turn it and till it by our own labor." It is largely a private effort, although government bears responsibility to help this and similar undertakings, given the restrictive covenants that barred Richardson's predecessors.

One such program operates in the City of Detroit through the Detroit Land Bank Authority, which has a best-in-class mechanism to offer vacant properties for sale to residents, community organizations, developers, and others. The inventory includes properties that revert to the city through tax foreclosure, as well as city properties that are deemed surplus. The city sells these sites for uses that will not only benefit the public but also restore the properties to productive functions. Baltimore and other places need similar structures, and to facilitate greater diversity among buyers. Local, state, and federal policies could bolster these endeavors. From land banks to development funds, Black taxpayers deserve effective government services that address communities' needs. Together with private actors like Richardson, these components form the essential spokes of a unified wheel driving collective business growth and development.

In December 2023, Richardson brought back the Edmondson Village holiday light celebration that had been terminated years before.[16] On a chilly Friday night, hundreds savored the renewed celebration, complete with a grand tree, warm food, hot cocoa, and photo opportunities with Santa.

"To see the village come back to life is a treat," the same Edmondson Village resident, Lashelle Bynum, told ABC affiliate WMAR Channel 2. "I mean, just seeing the lamp poles lit, brings back a memory for me. I've been here since the sixties."

Bynum, who took photos to preserve the moment, continued, "To me this gives me hope for the new beginning that I see coming, and as far as me taking photos, this is home for me, so I want to capture home."

BUSINESS-BUILT BLACK POWER

As a child, when asked about his dream career, Kalen Hodgest toggled between lawyering and dentistry. Both professions fascinated him, yet it wasn't the allure of courtroom battles or the science of smiles that called to him; it was the idea of autonomy. Kalen's goals weren't aimed at joining an established firm or medical practice. Instead, he conjured a mission to work for himself. "I've always seen myself being my boss," he told me. "Being an entrepreneur has always been in me."

In the bustling city of St. Louis, Missouri, Kalen was an ordinary teenager who might have been dismissed as a kid running side hustles. In fact, he was displaying the same entrepreneurial spirit that brings C-suite executives applause, but with significantly less resources. His parents were supportive of his endeavors but didn't have the kind of capital that went beyond providing a nurturing and loving home and a lawn mower. His dad was incarcerated for most of his childhood. His mother worked for the local cable company and then for the Veterans Administration.

His circumstances seemingly cultivated his drive. As early as thirteen he began washing cars and tinting windows at a neighborhood car wash to earn money. He saved his earnings to buy himself a car at sixteen, which he traded in for a truck shortly after.

With his family's lawn mower in the back of his truck, Kalen began his first business venture. What started as a service for family and friends soon had him cruising the streets of his hometown, taming unruly yards under the midwestern sun. The money didn't come fast enough to grow his company, so to add revenue Kalen worked nights at the post office. Soon, he had saved enough to purchase additional equipment and hire other people. At sixteen, he became what most business owners don't achieve until much later in life, if ever—an employer.

This is where Kalen's story begins. It's not a familiar account of someone turning a lawn-mowing business into a health-care company, a restaurant, a logistics start-up, or a real estate development firm. It's a testament to the seed of entrepreneurship that can grow within a determined Black community.

* * *

BUSINESS OWNERSHIP LIES at the heart of the American dream, the belief in equal opportunity for prosperity, success, and upward mobility, regardless of background or circumstances, through hard work and determination. Business ownership represents the freedom to provide for oneself and one's family. Americans collectively envision self-sufficiency and self-determination as a free-market system in which anyone can start a business to support their family. Businesses may also be incubators of innovation and technology, which contribute as drivers of sustained improvements in living standards.[1] Americans collectively believe in the power of free enterprise. However, our faith in free markets has not always been matched by our commitment to free people.

Warren Buffett is generally credited with saying, "Someone is sitting in the shade today because someone planted a tree a long time ago." Some interpret the quote as a testament to diligence and patience in making long-term investments. Others think it illustrates the idea that entrepreneurial labor and determination lay the groundwork for freedom and security. But one can also read the Buffett quote literally, as referring to the privileges that stemmed from centuries of slavery and Jim Crow racism.

Under chattel slavery, Black people were themselves a market—bought, traded, and mortgaged—and they were prohibited from formally engaging in local, regional, or global enterprise. Instead, they planted the trees that provided shade for others. There was some commercial activity among people in bondage: in their restricted free time, they made handicrafts and grew food in their gardens to trade or sell in urban marketplaces in locales like Charleston, Savannah, and New Orleans.[2] Many worked beyond their indentured labor, saved, and bought themselves out of slavery.

But Black people were excluded from participating in free markets until the passage of the Thirteenth Amendment in 1865 and the Civil Rights Act of 1866, which codified their right to "make and enforce contracts, to sue, be parties, and give evidence, to inherit, purchase, lease, sell, hold, and convey real and personal property." Still, for decades thereafter, Black Americans had to contend with a culture that did not consider them equal under law, let alone part of free enterprise.

At a Martin Luther King Jr. Day event in 2023, Treasury Secretary Janet Yellen said, "From Reconstruction, to Jim Crow, to the present day, our economy has never worked fairly for Black Americans—or, really, for any American of color."[3] Beyond slavery, Yellen's remarks were an acknowledgment that US policymakers had established racially tilted rules for the economy, prohibiting business and wealth development among Black Americans, along with many other harms. So, for the descendants of enslaved Africans in the United States, entrepreneurship represents more than simply owning a business and reaping financial benefits. It also means true membership in a country that denied them access to the American dream.

If Black people's freedom is linked to their ability to create and sell products in the marketplace, to engage in free enterprise, then they must also have full access to all that makes that possible. We might take the rate of Black employers, those able to hire others, as a primary indicator of racial progress. So, by this measure, how is the United States progressing?

As discussed, the rate of business ownership among Black individuals in a county or metro area serves as a relatively modest yet meaningful indicator of life expectancy. As the Black Progress Index database showed, approximately 1 percent of Black adults aged eighteen to sixty-four own an employer business, and good economic conditions for business seem to coincide with what's good for health. However, as a proportion of the US population, Black business ownership is significantly lower than that of other racial groups.

The numbers bear repeating: in 2021, Black individuals made up 14.4 percent of the population,[4] but they owned only 2.7 percent of all businesses with employees, according to a Brookings analysis of the US Census Annual Business Survey.[5] White individuals owned 82 percent of employer businesses, but they represented 72.5 percent of the population. Asian individuals owned 10.9 percent of employer businesses despite making up 6.3 percent of the population. For both Latino or Hispanic business owners and Native owners, business ownership percentages were lower than their respective shares of the population. Latino or Hispanic business owners represented 6.9 percent of employer businesses while comprising 19 percent of the population. Similarly, Native owners held 0.8 percent of employer businesses but represented 2.6 percent of the population.

The share of Black-owned sole proprietorships—businesses without employees—were closer to the share of the population, representing 12.7 of all sole proprietorships, for a total of 3.5 million businesses. These make up a disproportionately high share of Black-owned businesses overall: 96.3 percent. This is more than the share of white (81.1 percent), Asian American (80.1 percent), Latino or Hispanic (92.4 percent), and Native (92.4 percent) businesses.

In 2024, Gallup researchers created an index of personality traits that are highly predictive of whether workers will become entrepreneurs.[6] It measures the extent of workers' "a) non-cognitive skills, such as conscientiousness, emotional stability, and determination; b) internal locus of control, meaning that they direct and influence their lives; c) entrepreneurial and operational self-efficacy, meaning confidence that they could perform the activities associated with starting and running a business; and d) desire for autonomous, creative work that matches their natural talents." These are intangible traits associated with being successful in business. Gallup assessed them among white, Black, Hispanic, and multiracial adults, who were highly educated, older workers. They found that more than a quarter—or 27 percent—of Black adults with jobs have very high scores on the index. Yet, of these people, less than 1 percent run a company with employees and 74 percent do not own a company, which is out of line with the findings for other racial groups.

There are no doubt millions of Kalens who have yet to match their attributes with the career to which they are most suited—entrepreneurship. Because of lower levels of wealth, limited access to debt capital, and discrimination, Black people who are built to be entrepreneurs are more likely not to live up to their potential. But what they colloquially refer to as "hustle" to describe how the Kalens of the community operate encapsulates the attributes of entrepreneurialism.

When Black employers do start their own firms, they have a much harder time scaling them because of restrictions that keep them from reaching their potential. In the same Gallup study, researchers found that Black and Hispanic business owners encounter more obstacles and unfair treatment more frequently than white or Asian business owners when trying to access capital and attract customers. Most people start their firms using personal wealth. Black and Hispanic owners on average start with much less. In 2022, median Black wealth stood at approximately $45,000, $62,000 for nonwhite Hispanics; $285,000 for whites; and $536,000 for Asian American households.

If you don't have wealth to draw upon, debt capital become the other option. However, 70 percent of Black and 58 percent of Hispanic business proprietors who applied for financing in 2023 found it "challenging," whereas this was the case for only 40 percent of white and 32 percent of Asian owners. On another survey item, Black and Hispanic proprietors were three to four times likelier to perceive unfair treatment during the financing process than their white and Asian counterparts. In contrast, an overwhelming majority of white (96 percent) and Asian (97 percent) business owners reported receiving fair treatment when seeking financing, unlike 84 percent of Black and 87 percent of Hispanic business owners.

For this reason, Black people see discrimination as a barrier to becoming an employer. Although they have the traits, drive, and creativity, they are lacking—and are owed—the capital they were prohibited from accumulating through business development, homeownership, and investing.

While raising the share of employer firms to equal or exceed the proportion of Black people in the United States is a path to power, this book rejects racialized capitalism and reproducing the business practices that have entrenched Black people in the lower echelons of society. Instead, the goal of utilizing business as a tool for Black empowerment is to foster equal opportunity and engagement in markets, and to achieve these aims through innovation. Black individuals have consistently endeavored to innovate the markets themselves, liberating all people from discrimination.

An entrepreneur such as Chris Bennett of Miami aims to do more than build a successful early childcare company—Bennett focused on transforming the industry for the communities that need childcare. He created Wonderschool, a virtual platform and business model that helps parents both find and start their own childcare centers, guiding them to provide quality, affordability, and access for providers and consumers. Ruben Harris founded Career Karma, a platform to assist people seeking to enter the often exclusive field of technology by connecting applicants with bootcamps, mentors, and networks. The success of these kinds of market and industry innovations are evident in the data. According to a 2023 Brookings report analyzing the Annual Business Survey, Black women and men were most motivated by a collective mission. Over 75 percent of Black women and 73 percent of Black men listed "wanting to help my community" as a key factor when deciding to start a new business. This is 15 percent and 13 percent higher than the average for all entrepreneurs and over 18 percent and 13 percent higher than for white men, who were the least likely to cite this as an influential factor.

* * *

MOWING LAWNS WASN'T the breadth of Kalen's ambition. At sixteen, he was already diversifying, tapping into the city's musical pulse with a business burning CDs, which helped him purchase his first car. Kalen would bounce from barbershop to salon selling copies of the most popular hip-hop and R&B albums of the day. His enterprising journey took another twist when a proposition came along. "Someone approached me about putting the CDs at a store location. We could sell candy and music," Kalen recollects. Using the money he made from selling CDs, Kalen contributed his resources to join his partners, who had their own capital, to set up a convenience store, a venture filled with aspiration that would be tempered by real-world lessons in the challenges of partnership.

The store lasted only four or five months before it veered off course, but Kalen kept on juggling CD sales, his landscaping business, and his job at the post office, developing skills along the way. His ventures swept him across St. Louis, from barbershops, where he peddled his CDs, to yards in every nook of the city and county. His tenacity set the rhythm of his days, each one strategically organized to advance a future built on the bedrock of self-made success.

When Kalen was introduced to the business of health care by his father's friends, he shifted direction. These family friends may not have had large sums of investment capital, but they were role models who could offer guiding hands. The fact that they worked in health care is not coincidental—many Black entrepreneurs have gravitated toward opportunities created by the need for improved health outcomes. According to the 2020 Brookings study of employer firms, the health care and social assistance industry represented the largest share of Black-owned employer businesses, at nearly one-third. This was followed by professional, scientific, and technical services, which represented 14.8 percent of Black employers; this broad category includes engineering, veterinary services, and specialized design—all jobs that require technical training. The third-largest industry was administrative, support, and waste management and remediation services, which represented 8.2 percent of Black-owned employer businesses.

A friend of Kalen's father worked as a consultant in health-care services, helping aspiring home-care providers develop business plans and operation materials, understand state budgeting, and create internal structures. The family friend allowed Kalen to shadow her for a month and learn the ropes of the industry. She connected him with other health-care management consultants who assisted him drafting paperwork and proposals to offer nursing assistance and transportation, cleaning, and therapeutic services. He began to formulate a vision for a health-care company, relying on his mentors, who were pivotal in drawing up the business plan for the home health agency he eventually submitted to the state. Kalen's next step was college, where he studied health-care administration, aligning his academic work with his aspirations. But as his health-care business gained traction, Kalen faced a crossroads. His real-world experience began to eclipse his formal education, and his enterprise demanded more attention. So he made the bold decision to leave college after taking a few classes and devote himself fully to his blossoming company.

The 2024 Gallup index found that the connection between educational achievement and business ownership is not all that strong. Individuals with a bachelor's degree are only slightly more likely to be proprietors compared to all workers (1.9 percent versus 1.7 percent), while those who hold master's degrees are less likely to be owners (1.4 percent). At the same time, rates of owning a nonemployer firm and being self-employed are greater among less educated workers than those who are highly educated.

Kalen launched his health-care company at nineteen, securing a contract with Medicaid through the Missouri Department of Health and Senior Services. His company provided homemaker services—cooking, cleaning, transportation, and more—to support seniors in the comfort of their homes, fulfilling a mission to enable them to live independently for as long as possible.

Kalen recalls, "The health-care company was my most formalized business—that was the first time I really got consistent with having customers and a few employees. All my cousins worked with me, helping me out."

The fledgling firm, devoted to dignity and care, saw remarkable growth. From generating about $110,000 in its first year, the company swiftly escalated to revenues surpassing seven figures in the next two, a testament to Kalen's dedication and the profound need for compassionate health-care services in the area. As we have seen—either directly, through services provided, or indirectly, by way of improved economic conditions in neighborhoods—business ownership is correlated with health and wealth, two components of Black power.

* * *

THE CAUSAL MECHANISM for the connection is unclear. One 2018 study published in the *Journal of Urbanism* asserted that enhancing economic conditions for business is also good for the development of individuals and communities.[7] The logic seems straightforward. The authors suggest that in regions where there are "more and stronger local small businesses," the internal economic connections within the community are more robust, there is a greater availability of local jobs, and the economies are more affluent overall. These favorable economic situations correlate with reduced crime rates, fewer injuries, increased opportunities for physical activity, and improved access to healthcare services, all of which collectively enhance the prospects for a community's residents to lead healthier and longer lives. Nonetheless, the study cautioned that health benefits associated with small-business ownership and community development are not guaranteed or equitable.

To establish conditions that foster these benefits, the 2018 study stated that deliberate measures and, often, specific investments are essential. Access to capital, business education, and networking opportunities often remain out of reach or are challenging to secure for certain entrepreneurs, particularly immigrants, people of color, those in rural areas, and those operating in low-income neighborhoods, due to barriers to traditional private lending sources. Public funding directed toward technical assistance and financial resources can bridge this gap, enabling small businesses to launch, stabilize, expand, and drive local economic enhancement. Consequently, bolstering small-business support in traditionally underresourced areas holds the potential to offer extensive health benefits by fostering economic opportunities within these communities.

*   *   *

AMONG THE 135 metropolitan areas surveyed between 2017 and 2021, 76 percent experienced growth in Black-owned employer businesses. Southern metropolitan regions saw the most significant rise, but these figures still did not match the demographic proportion of Black residents in these locales. All of the ten metro areas with the top rates of Black employer business ownership were in the Southeast, including four in the state of Georgia. Despite Fayetteville, North Carolina, leading these areas with 12.4 percent of employer businesses being Black owned, this was still considerably less than the Black population, which was 36.4 percent of the city's residents.

The raw numbers were highest in larger metropolises, such as New York City, with 16,506 Black-owned businesses making up 3.5 percent of all employer businesses, and Chicago, where 5,606 businesses comprised 2.8 percent of the total. While St. Louis had the tenth-largest quantity of Black-owned employer businesses in 2021, it also saw a stark decline, losing 3,205, or more than half, since 2017—a drop more severe than in any other surveyed city.

It's unclear what has caused the growth of Black-owned business, but increased capital from COVID-19 stimulus funds played a role, alleviating the difficulty Black entrepreneurs experience when seeking credit. The rise in Black-owned employer firms continued during the pandemic. According to our analysis of the Census Bureau's Annual Business Survey, the number grew consecutively from 2017 to 2021, up by 14 percent, which may come as a surprise. But entrepreneurs seemed to invest COVID relief stimulus dollars and take advantage of the increased discretionary time to start new firms, many of them in health care to meet the needs of the Black community, given its higher rates of COVID.

The link between the growth of business and better health outcomes is explained by another factor, which is increased wealth. Net housing equity drove the largest portion of wealth accumulation for Black Americans from 2019 to 2022. The second-most significant driver of wealth was equity from businesses, which represented 21 percent of wealth accumulation for Black households. The proportion of business equity in wealth was much lower for Latino or Hispanic households (4 percent) but similar for white households (22 percent) and other non-Latino or Hispanic groups (21 percent).

To understand the role of socioeconomic factors and their influence on health, a group of researchers in 2007 did a systematic review of twenty-nine studies from 1990 to 2006.[8] The consensus indicated that greater wealth is generally associated with better health outcomes, even when adjusting for other socioeconomic metrics. This association was particularly strong in the studies that incorporated detailed measures of assets and debts. Additionally, accounting for wealth often revealed a decrease in health disparities related to race and ethnicity, suggesting that wealth measurements could provide more nuanced insights into how socioeconomic factors affect health.

Clearly, an increase in Black businesses can play a critical role in enhancing wealth, and not just for business owners but also for community members, due to job creation. In 2020, Black businesses employed 1.3 million people and created over 48,000 new jobs.

*   *   *

As KALEN's HEALTH-CARE company grew, he began looking into starting a logistics business as an Amazon delivery
service partner, providing vans and drivers to deliver packages. Once again, this venture was partly inspired by family
members and friends who were starting similar ventures at
around the same time, including a relative who mentioned,
"Hey, you know Amazon's making some money," as Kalen
recalled.

Having the support of family with business experience
seems to be a boost for most entrepreneurs. The 2024 Gallup study looked at the parents of business owners, the parents' financial stability during childhood, and the highest
level of education attained by either parent. Of these factors, having a family business was the most significant predictor of future ownership—2.4 percent versus 1.3 percent
of owners whose families did not have their own business.
Additionally, the rate of self-employment is slightly elevated
among workers whose parents were business owners.

Using the capital and wealth from all of his other ventures, Kalen secured a contract with Amazon, and his logistics company oversees an operation involving sixty vans
and approximately ninety employees, primarily managed
by his wife. After ten years of developing the health-care
company, which had helped secure the capital to start the
logistics venture, Kalen sold it to focus on his new enterprise and step into real estate development.

Amid all his other endeavors, Kalen opened a restaurant in the heart of St. Louis, in the lively hum of one of

its most vibrant neighborhoods. Putting his past success to work, Kalen bought the property, a former coffee shop, at a steal in 2015 and originally operated his health-care business out of the building. While there, he developed a vision for a restaurant, Bait, which opened in 2019 to great fanfare. One *Riverfront Times* review was titled, "Bait Stuns with an Upscale Approach to Seafood."[9] The writer gushed over the restaurant's decor: "Hodgest spared no expense when it comes to Bait's aesthetics. True to his vision for a swanky spot, Bait is a monumental departure from the space's former occupants." The praise continued: "Less a seafood restaurant than a temple to the ocean's bounty, Bait dazzles with presentations that come up to the line of over-the-top without ever crossing them."

The new establishment initially proved successful. Kalen served delectable dishes to a consistent customer base. However, COVID-19 and a soured relationship with his business partner led Kalen to conclude that the restaurant was no longer worth the thrill. Shutting it down led to an intriguing evolution. Aware that he had a valuable asset in the heart of a thriving St. Louis neighborhood, Kalen decided to lease it to a new operator. The space was transformed into a fragrance bar, a place where customers could create signature scents. Kalen described it as a "sip and paint" venue with a twist: guests make fragrances and enjoy small bites and charcuterie. He kept the kitchen operational for catering jobs and to provide food for the fragrance bar. The reinvention was not only fresh and revitalizing but also a smart move, as Kalen continued to diversify his revenue streams.

Though no longer a restaurateur, Kalen leveraged his

new endeavor to expand into real estate. He took what he had learned from creating a restaurant and applied it to housing. "My development company is in its infancy," he said. "We started about a year ago, focusing on market rate and low-income apartments, along with multi-family housing developments." Kalen has approximately ten projects of varying sizes, including a low-income housing project (acquired through city tax credits), fifty senior apartments, and a commercial construction in North St. Louis.

When it comes to scaling, in many ways Kalen is a role model for Black business growth. He scaled his ventures by building upon them, multiple enterprises at a time. He is not alone. In 2021, the count of Black employers surged by 14.3 percent over the previous year, an increase greater than any other racial group, according to data from the Census Bureau's Annual Business Survey. That same year, Black-owned employer businesses exhibited the most significant growth in terms of employees (7 percent), revenue (30 percent), and payroll (27 percent) compared to other employer businesses.

However, even if Black business ownership continued to grow at that rate, it would take another eighty years to reach parity with the Black population share. If we assume an expansion in the economy such that no gains in Black business revenue or size came at the expense of non-Black businesses, it would take an additional 682,000 Black-owned employer businesses to equal the share of Black individuals in 2021—representing an estimated $776 billion more in revenue and the creation of 5.9 million jobs.

One approach is to grow a company like Kalen's by leveraging the capital from one business venture for the next. But investors can help accelerate growth by recognizing the strength of business owners such as Kalen. Instead, Black businesses are often taken for granted. At a community level, they are devalued and prejudged simply for being in predominantly Black neighborhoods. According to the 2020 Brookings study mentioned earlier, highly rated businesses—measured by five-star ratings on Yelp—located in Black-majority neighborhoods experience an annual reduction in business revenue totaling up to $3.9 billion, seemingly in relation to the perception of Black people in proximity to the business. In other words, we would expect those highly rated businesses to gain $3.9 billion in revenue if they were located in white neighborhoods. As noted, these financial realities contrast with the findings that Black-, Brown-, and Asian-owned businesses receive customer reviews of equal quality to those of white-owned businesses.

Many neighborhood businesses are just as good, but they don't get fair consideration and consequently get less revenue. Dismantling the trap of negative perceptions requires investment in these underappreciated assets, which would grow if they received proper support. That growth would ultimately lead to greater development for the businesses as well as the communities they serve.

Too often, grant and loan programs put Black entrepreneurs through financial literacy training and other educational support programs, assuming there are holes needing to be filled. Given our Yelp review study, we can assume that Black, Latino, and Asian owners don't lack business acumen or need any more training than white entrepreneurs. Certainly, continuous learning helps businesspeople keep pace in a technologically driven society. But what Black businesses need is capital.

Those with a deficit perspective tend to see lower outcomes as the result of character flaws and social gaps, so they avoid investing in people in ways that build on their strengths. Nothing grows without investment, and no one invests in problems alone. Thus cities must prioritize investing in their strengths.

Venture capitalists are notorious for failing to see Black firms as scalable, although venture capital enables the hiring of employees, purchase of equipment, and development of systems to accelerate business growth. Kalen's business isn't the type that venture capitalists typically seek. They did invest in Chris Bennett's Wonderschool and Ruben Harris's Career Karma, both of which were tech firms. Venture capitalists, representing less than a percent of all financial assets, typically invest in Silicon Valley tech firms but also in biomedical technologies and other businesses that are built for the kind of rapid and substantive revenue growth that disrupts markets. For instance, Rihanna's lingerie line, Savage X Fenty, raised $115 million in funding at a valuation of $1 billion. Neighborhood-facing businesses are not targets for venture capital, and there is some overlap in how those businesses and Black-owned firms are viewed.

Boosted by television shows and competitions like the popular *Shark Tank*, venture capital gets outsized attention given that fewer than 1 percent of US companies have raised capital from VC firms. And those businesses that do raise venture capital aren't very diverse. Washington University in St. Louis and the Brookings Institution did an analysis of venture capital distribution and found that only 2 percent of venture capital funds were directed toward start-ups with exclusively female founding teams in the United States, despite women comprising 50.5 percent of the population.[10] Similarly, Black founders received a mere 1 percent of venture capital funding in 2020 and 1.4 percent in 2021, despite constituting approximately 14 percent of the population. Similarly, Hispanic or Latinx individuals and Native Americans received disproportionately minimal shares of venture capital funding.

There are new and emerging financial service companies that recognize the value in overlooked founders, including those who are Black, Latino, and Indigenous. These companies are using diversity as a competitive advantage to generate positive returns for investors. Zeal Capital is a venture capital firm that invests in companies with diverse management teams aiming to close wealth, skills, and health-care gaps. Among the thirty firms in their portfolio are Esusu, which helps tenants monitor their credit scores and assists landlords in lowering evictions and filling vacancies through data and technology, and GigEasy, which provides insurance infrastructure for the gig economy, enabling platforms and businesses to offer commercial insurance and benefits to their workers.

For capital to go beyond the less than 1 percent that VC firms provide, society needs traditional capital allocators to reach diverse founders. A fuller financial service firm, Known, is a Black, Indigenous, Latina, and Asian American–owned allocator that leverages the capital of its clients (institutions, endowments, and large family offices) by investing in demographics that Wall Street typically overlooks, where they see the potential for massive growth.

According to its website, "Known is building a 'mothership' to provide the funding, counsel, technology, and back-office support needed to grow BIPOC-owned asset management firms, businesses and investment funds to their rightful scale." For businesses to scale, banks, credit unions, and community development financial organizations must generate loans and mortgages, investment firms must provide capital to VCs like Zeal, and retirement funds must be directed by people who see the potential in Black, Latino, and Native American led firms. In St. Louis, investment in Black businesses to bring them to parity with the Black share of the population in the metro area—19.5 percent—would create 9,346 more Black employer firms.

There are currently 3,003 Black employers, accounting for just 5.9 percent of employer businesses in the St. Louis metropolitan area. Black businesses create an average of six jobs per firm, compared to an average of twenty-two for all businesses in the area. If the average number of employees per Black business reached parity, it would create approximately 47,653 new jobs. And if the number of Black businesses matched the population size and the employees per firm matched the average business, it would create 252,522 jobs. Additionally, Black businesses pay their employees an average of $30,805, compared to an average of $60,834 per employee for all businesses in St. Louis. If Black businesses paid this much, then their employees would see an increase in total pay of approximately $545,702,250.

There are organizations committed to boosting the representation of Black employers. Path to 15|55, a national collaborative effort led by the organization CapEQ involving professionals from various fields and sectors, aims to foster the growth of Black enterprises and their communities.[11] The initiative is underpinned by research indicating that if merely 15 percent of Black-owned businesses could expand to employ just one additional worker, the US economy has the potential to increase by $55 billion. Path to 15|55 has leveraged $100 million in corporate commitments dedicated to the growth of Black businesses, applied to supporting policy changes at various government levels and to investing in Black businesses. The Path 15|55 fund employs a collective strategy by connecting Black-led and -influenced capital initiatives with investors, nonprofits, government agencies, and financial institutions. This strategy aims to share and scale innovations in risk methodologies, provide flexible capital sources, fuel high-growth industries, and enhance place-based infrastructure, thereby ensuring sustainable systems for Black business growth. In the Brookings publication *The Public Wealth of Cities*, Dag Detter and Stefan Fölster propose the adoption of Urban Wealth Funds, which would operate as publicly owned private equity funds that utilize existing investments by the city. Enhancing this idea to include an explicit commitment to businesses owned by Black people would be a step toward closing the gap in access to capital that could be used to scale businesses and generate returns for cities as well.[12]

Capital can be deployed in very specific ways. As mentioned, Black entrepreneurs are underrepresented across various types of employer firms. Attaining business equity relies on the expansion of high-revenue sectors, a goal that presents a significantly greater challenge than it does in industries where Black individuals already have higher representation. In 2018, for example, there were a mere eighteen Black businesses in the utilities sector in the United States. Industries such as utilities, wholesale trade, and manufacturing, which generate substantial revenue, require significant start-up capital.[13] In these industries, a targeted approach is essential to bolster the presence of Black enterprise.

Allocating funds to prioritized industries is a strategic move given their potential for expansion. Among these, health care and social assistance firms stand out as promising sectors. The demand, resulting especially from the COVID-19 pandemic, for skilled professionals and businesses in health care and related fields created opportunities to invest in Black firms in these vital areas. Supporting Black entrepreneurs in ventures ranging from the development of health-care technologies to the recruitment of contact tracers would present a dual advantage, by fostering the growth of these enterprises and aiding the nation in navigating through future health-care crises.

Targeted place-based investments can build on existing momentum. Addressing the undervaluation of residences and businesses in Black neighborhoods would involve creating incentives to attract consumer-focused enterprises and high-growth businesses to operate within these communities. Economic vitality is increasingly centered in major metropolitan regions, aligning with the concentrations of Black populations. While St. Louis boasts a substantial presence of Black-owned businesses and a commendable level of demographic representation among business owners, enabling Black businesses to thrive requires enhanced visibility and participation in larger urban centers.

The COVID-19 crisis starkly revealed the deep-seated impacts of systemic racism, evidenced by the disproportionately high Black mortality rates. While the virus itself does not discriminate, the existing structures and policies related to housing, health care, and business play a pivotal role in shaping neighborhood dynamics and market disparities, ultimately influencing outcomes. An illustration of this disparity was seen in the initial distribution of Paycheck Protection Program (PPP) loans as part of the Coronavirus Aid, Relief, and Economic Security (CARES) Act, which predominantly favored employer firms. This approach significantly overlooked Black-owned businesses, as the majority operate as nonemployer companies, contrasting sharply with their white-owned counterparts.

Moreover, the analysis of PPP loan distribution revealed geographic biases: a higher concentration of funds were allocated to white-majority congressional districts compared to districts where nonwhite minorities represent the majority. This disparity underscored the financial institutions' failure to connect effectively with the Black community, emphasizing the urgent need for stronger relationships between Black businesses and banks to ensure their sustainability. Efforts aimed at reducing the number of unbanked Black businesses and households must be prioritized to promote financial inclusion and resilience within the community.

Strategic procurement initiatives that aim to increase the participation of Black businesses in government and large corporate contracts can significantly boost the growth trajectory of these firms. By implementing inclusive procurement practices, both public entities and corporations can foster an environment conducive to the advancement of Black-owned enterprises.

In New Orleans, for example, despite being in the majority, Black residents historically faced exclusion from local government contracting opportunities. To address this disparity, leaders in the region committed to prioritizing underserved populations. A notable example is the regional transit authority in New Orleans, which took proactive measures to support both infrastructure development and businesses owned by individuals of color. By ensuring that a minimum of 31 percent of federally allocated grants are directed toward contracts with certified minority-owned businesses, the transit authority is actively promoting economic empowerment and opportunity within the community.

For centuries, Black people were robbed of the opportunity to develop wealth, resulting in less capital to scale and develop businesses. What is owed is the capital, but what is promised is growth. Kalen's projects blossomed one after the other—from his lawn-mowing business to his health-care firm and real estate development company. Kalen is an asset to North St. Louis. He built his businesses on a foundation of aspirations, resolve, family support, and skill. More than humble beginnings, these attributes exist in abundance in Black communities, ready to put capital to work.

5

GETTING TO CLOSING

The power to live is inextricably linked to homeownership. Based on findings from the Black Progress Index, the Black homeownership rate in a county or metro area is highly predictive of length of life: for every standard increase in those rates, the average life is extended by 0.61 years. The places that exhibit the highest rates of Black homeowners in an area is associated with an increase in how long people live there.

The counties that exhibit the highest rates of Black homeownership are Hancock County in Indiana, with a 96.0 percent homeownership rate and a life expectancy estimate of 83.0 years, and New Kent County in Virginia, with a 92.1 percent homeownership rate and a life expectancy estimate of 77.5 years, surpassing the national average of 74 years.

There are exceptions to the trend, such as Clarke and Jasper Counties in Mississippi, where despite high Black homeownership rates of 78.4 percent and 78.2 percent, the life expectancy estimates are below the national average.

This suggests that additional factors, such as economic opportunities, health-care access, and social support systems, also play significant roles. Nevertheless, homeownership, with its connection to wealth, is strongly associated with health: wealthier people live longer, so there are few other targets for Black power movements that are as important.

The relationship of homeownership in the United States to political and economic systems means that it has significant bearing on the state of our democracy, affecting representation, growth, and funding for municipal services such as education and policing. The substantial social and economic benefits of homeownership are also evident in greater educational achievement, heightened civic engagement, lower crime rates, and decreased dependence on public assistance for those who live in the home.[1] From a psychological perspective, owning a home is linked to greater life satisfaction and improved mental well-being.

Presidents have reinforced the crucial role of homeownership. In 1931, at the Annual Convention of Building and Loan Associations, President Herbert Hoover said, "Home owning is more than the provision of domiciles; it goes to the roots of family life, public morals and standards of living."[2] During a roundtable discussion with housing industry representatives in 1984, Ronald Reagan stated, "Home ownership is an essential part of the American dream, fundamental to our way of life." President George W. Bush said plainly, "Owning a home is a part of that dream, it just is. Right here in America, if you own your own home, you're realizing the American dream."[3] In a 2013 speech at a Phoenix, Arizona, high school, President Barack Obama

referred to homeownership as "the most tangible cornerstone that lies at the heart of the American dream." He
added, a "home is the ultimate evidence that here in America, hard work pays off, that responsibility is rewarded."[4]

Despite tethering homeownership to citizenship, legal
racial discrimination was codified in housing markets
throughout much of America's history, posing an obstacle
that prevented Black people from becoming full-fledged
members of society. Discriminatory systems prevalent
during segregation are normalized features of today's housing markets, such as racially biased zoning ordinances, housing covenants, and insurance underwriting. Practices such as
single-family zoning ordinances (which shut out occupants
whose income level demands smaller, multifamily dwellings)
and the sales comparison approach to appraisals (which
undervalue Black-owned housing) continue to exist, shaping outcomes today.

A 2023 Harvard study showed that the homeownership
rate among white households stood at 72 percent, contrasting with approximately 42 percent for Black households.[5]
Racial differences also exist at every age group across the
lifespan. In 2019, the treasury reported that households
headed by white individuals consistently maintained
homeownership rates at least 10 percentage points above
those of Black and Hispanic households, irrespective of the
age of the household head.

Awareness of the detrimental long-term effect of discriminatory policies such as redlining has gradually reached
mainstream recognition. By identifying areas with significant
Black populations (marking them with red ink on maps),
banks sent a warning signal to mortgage lenders, resulting in

a lack of credit and diminished levels of investment in segregated Black neighborhoods.[6] Whiter or less-Black neighborhoods became intrinsically better and more valuable. The vestiges of this discrimination are evident in lower home values in Black areas, robbing individuals and communities of wealth.[7]

In 2018, my colleagues Jonathan Rothwell, David Harshbarger, and I showed in a Brookings Institution report that homes of similar quality in neighborhoods with similar amenities are worth 23 percent less in majority-Black neighborhoods than in neighborhoods with very few or no Black residents. This percentage equates to Black homeowners being deprived of $48,000 per home, amounting to about $156 billion in lost equity nationwide. To put that in perspective, given the average capital Black people use to start their firms, the lost worth would support more than 4.4 million new businesses. It would cover tuition for more than eight million four-year degrees from public institutions. The cumulative loss would have covered all the damage from Hurricane Katrina and replaced the lead pipes in Flint, Michigan, three thousand times over.

Accruing equity through homeownership is the most common pathway to wealth among all racial groups in the country, but it is the greatest source of wealth creation for Black families. Based on the Federal Reserve's Survey of Consumer Finances, 19 percent of all growth in wealth for Black people in 2022 came from housing equity, followed by business equity at 6 percent. This is compared to 5 percent and 11 percent for white and Hispanic families, respectively.

With Black wealth highly concentrated in housing,

Black overall worth ebbs and flows with the housing market. For this reason Black wealth increased during the COVID-19 pandemic, Brookings found, in a period when housing prices soared.[8] However, the racial wealth gap also increased in the same period, due to stock market gains, which led to significant financial growth for white and Asian families, given their greater investments in securities.

There's a place for a discussion on diversifying Black wealth sources, but a practical approach to building wealth should begin with leveraging existing assets. Black power movements should focus on increasing homeownership rates, setting a specific goal: 75 percent would represent parity with white homeowners. Reaching that goal requires significant changes to the housing landscape, including increasing inventory, to dismantle the historic discrimination baked into so many facets of policy.

According to a 2024 Zillow report, there is a notable disparity between Black and white families in mortgage readiness, with 7.8 percent of Black nonhomeowning families having income that makes them ready for a mortgage, compared to 12.5 percent of white families, reflecting a 4.7 percentage point gap.[9] However, this gap has decreased by over one-third since 2012, when it stood at 7.9 percentage points. Out of the housing crisis of 2008, poverty has declined among Black people and more are in the middle class, qualifying for mortgages. Estimates by the Census Bureau's American Community Survey of 2022 reveal the presence of 8,775,799 Black renter-occupied households; of these, approximately 684,512 families were deemed income-ready for a mortgage.

Cities such as Detroit, Memphis, St. Louis, Houston,

and Cleveland have high proportions of families renting who have sufficient income to comfortably afford a mortgage, ranging from 11.2 percent to 13.3 percent of renters. Nevertheless, despite the more affordable housing markets in these areas, challenges prevent broader access to homeownership.

When Black families seek to buy a house, they often find that the available mortgage options do not align with their economic reality. This forces many into taking loans that limit their financial flexibility, diminishing the benefits of owning a home. Past and present-day discrimination shows up in a lack or shortage of a down payment. Consequently, there's a need to create mortgage solutions tailored to the economic capacity of people who have experienced discrimination and to dismantle systemic obstacles, such as credit scoring and high wealth requirements, both of which limit access to credit.

Beyond the barriers to finance, Black power objectives for homeownership must focus on strategies to increase the supply of affordable housing, including changing zoning ordinances that will allow for multifamily units as well as increasing federal subsidies for building new units that can be owned. Black people live and work in many places with limited inventory, where there are simply fewer options to buy. Many Black communities face a shortage of quality housing stock, necessitating new construction. The scarcity of supply not only limits the choices for buyers, it also escalates demand, driving up prices.[10] Just as the federal government intervened to boost homeownership for white Americans through historic investments as part of the New Deal,[11] it could invest in construction to remedy lower wealth levels among Black families. However, a significant portion of tax incentives to build new homes often target rental property developers. Given the proliferation of Black renters who need to acquire assets to build wealth, innovative policies could promote and incentivize the development of multifamily homes, which could be purchased collectively.

Governmental and nongovernmental housing organizations could help remedy the impact of discrimination by developing cooperative ownership models to add to the conventional single-family concept. In these and other ways, policymakers must eliminate the vestiges of segregation and unleash the kind of innovation that Black homeowners need.

* * *

IN 2020, HOMEOWNERSHIP by Black households was at the same level as it was in 1968, when the Fair Housing Act, the federal antidiscrimination housing law, was enacted.[12] How have we made so little progress?

The answer is housing policy—or a lack thereof. Notwithstanding early versions of the Constitution, the American framework of inequality was perpetuated, as we have seen, through land ordinances and grants, racially restrictive housing covenants, Black codes, Jim Crow laws, the 1862 Homestead Act (awarding grants of government-surveyed land), the 1933 Home Owners' Loan Corporation Act (which sought to prevent defaulting on loans), the 1934 National Housing Act (making mortgages more affordable), urban renewal (which often displaced communities of color), and the National Interstate and Defense Highways

Act of 1956 (which also destroyed communities and enabled white flight), to name just a few practices.[13] Although the 1968 Fair Housing Act prohibited discrimination, theoretically putting an end to many of these policies, race-neutral aspects still exist.

A 2023 report by CNN revealed that Navy Federal Credit Union, the largest in the United States, had denied more than half of Black applicants for new conventional home mortgages in the previous year, while 75 percent of white applicants were approved for the same type of loan.[14] The report highlighted Navy Federal for having the largest gap in approval rates between Black and white borrowers among all major lenders that year. CNN's findings, derived from an analysis of public data from the government watchdog Consumer Financial Protection Bureau, also uncovered significant disparities in approval rates between Latino and white applicants.

Shortly after these allegations surfaced, a class-action lawsuit was filed against the credit union for discrimination, leading to immediate calls for a response.[15] California representative Maxine Waters, the leading Democrat on the House Financial Services Committee, demanded in a statement that "Navy Federal must explain both to Congress and their members how such practices took place, what immediate steps are being taken to correct the harm done, and who in management will be held accountable." Focusing scrutiny solely on one lender, however, could serve to absolve broader industry practices. Representative Waters's demand could just as well have extended to the whole housing industry.

CNN's analysis considered factors such as income,

debt-to-income ratios, property value, the percentage of down payment, and the nature of the neighborhood—aggregated information available on public databases. Responding to CNN, Navy Federal's spokesperson Bill Pearson criticized the report for presenting an inaccurate picture of the credit union's procedures, pointing out that the report overlooked "major criteria required by any financial institution to approve a mortgage loan," such as "credit score, available cash deposits and relationship history with the lender."[16]

Credit scores, which constitute a significant component of all lenders' underwriting practices, are not publicly available, which limited the CNN analysis. But as Lisa Rice and Deidre Swesnik, both with the National Fair Housing Alliance, explain in a 2012 article, "Discriminatory Effects of Credit Scoring on Communities of Color," those scores "do not just assess the risk characteristics of the borrower; they also reflect the riskiness of the environment in which a consumer is utilizing credit, as well as the riskiness of the types of products a consumer uses."[17] That makes them a legal vestige of our segregated past.

Some discriminatory lending practices are attributable to individual racism, which requires rigorous oversight to eliminate. But the broader issue of racial disparities in housing stems from standard practices and policies followed by all banks, which are seemingly neutral but disproportionately affect various groups. Changes to foundational aspects of the mortgage process could end that.

Innovations in credit scoring, such as the introduction of FICO 10T and VantageScore 4.0 in 2023, are steps forward. These models move away from the traditional approach of evaluating years' long credit reports and narrow the lens through which borrowers are assessed. FICO 10T examines credit behavior over at least twenty-four months, offering a more comprehensive view, while VantageScore allows for the consideration of shorter credit histories than the conventional FICO scores.

*   *   *

DON NASH, VICE president at the Homeownership Council of America, a national nonprofit dedicated to expanding homeownership and closing the wealth gap, is on a mission to tackle the racial disparity. "I started off in this business as a loan officer," Nash told me, detailing his evolution from selling loans to understanding the nuanced challenges in guiding a loan to the closing table. His transition from sales to an executive role allowed him to see the bigger picture of "systemic barriers" that "prevent many folks in the African American community from becoming homeowners."

Nash recognizes that the real risk to be mitigated in lending lies in the impact of past anti-Black policies on present-day individuals and families. He is attempting to do that by creating opportunities to leverage SPCPs in an imaginative way. SPCPs allow financial institutions to set up different credit options (down payment assistance, fee waivers, relaxing certain underwriting requirements) that help target special social needs. They are approved by the Equal Credit Opportunity Act and are designed to help specific groups of people who qualify as an "economically disadvantaged class of persons."[18] These programs may be authorized by federal or state laws, administered by non-profit organizations for their members or disadvantaged individuals, and can also be offered by for-profit organizations to meet special needs. SPCPs can be used by lenders in any sectors in which credit is extended, and the Department of Housing and Urban Development allows that SPCPs related to real estate loans or credit aid adhere to the Equal Credit Opportunity Act and are unlikely to breach the Fair Housing Act.

Nash sees a beacon of hope in SPCPs, which offer a range of supports, such as lower interest rates on loans, potentially saving homeowners thousands over the life of their mortgage, assistance with down payments, and support with closing costs. Money for down payment assistance comes from philanthropic foundations as well as commercial banks and lenders that become partners with the intention of gaining new customers. A family could receive $5,000 toward their down payment, or even up to $20,000 in areas with higher living costs. These tangible benefits directly address the economic hurdles that many people of color face.

Mortgage lenders can request and use specific relevant information to determine eligibility for an SPCP product. If financial need is a criterion, the creditor can consider adjusting typical elements of an application, like marital status, a spouse's financial resources, and other financial aspects to assess eligibility. An example of an SPCP is Bank of America's Community Affordable Loan Solution, launched in 2022, a new mortgage aimed at aiding first-time home buyers in majority-Black and -Brown communities.[19] It offers mortgages with zero down payment and zero closing costs, focusing initially on targeting neighborhoods in Charlotte, Dallas, Detroit, Los Angeles, and Miami.

To qualify as an SPCP, a program must meet certain criteria. It must have a written plan identifying the beneficiaries and outlining the procedures for providing credit. It should focus on extending credit to individuals who wouldn't typically qualify under normal credit standards or who would receive less favorable terms compared to other applicants. The Homeownership Council of America and other organizations, such as the National Fair Housing Alliance and the Mortgage Bankers Association, have launched toolkits designed for mortgage lenders looking to create SPCPs.[20]

Lisa Rice, president and CEO of NFHA, said in a statement that SPCP programs are an "excellent tool for expanding credit access for underserved markets, including consumers who live in credit deserts and are credit invisible." She added that SPCPs "help shore up long-standing inequities that have prevented equal access to economic prosperity."

At the heart of these organizations' guidance is evaluating loan production and performance metrics during the program's construction and monitoring phases. This approach helps ensure that an SPCP achieves its intended impact and stays compliant with federal and state laws.

Among the recommended metrics, lenders are advised to consider a spectrum of demographic, financial, and procedural considerations of borrowers: the area median income level, for example, to gauge economic diversity. Liquid assets at the time of closing and credit scores or alternative underwriting criteria offer lenses into the financial health and accessibility of the program for potential homeowners.

Further, good SPCPs monitor the geographic distribution of loans, focusing on low and moderate income levels, majority-minority census tracts, or both, to ensure equitable access across different communities. Scrutiny of borrower-paid closing costs, note rates (including any discounts applied through the program), and the loan terms underlines the importance of economic feasibility for participants. Additionally, monitoring housing types and the specific financial products utilized provides insight into the adaptability and responsiveness of SPCPs to diverse needs.

*   *   *

NASH, WHO IS based in Indianapolis, sees the need for effective SPCPs across the country. As someone who oversees programs and loan officers, he doesn't typically go out in the field, but some cases are too compelling for him to stay in the office. "I typically don't deal directly with consumers in the work that I do. But because we're consumer driven, you have to meet the people, hear the stories."

Nash recounted helping to bridge the gap between aspiration and reality for a Los Angeles family of six navigating uncertain times. "I'd gone to their apartment," he began, "just to meet with them, because they reached out and said, we heard you all have a program."

The father, a hardworking grip in the entertainment industry, faced an unexpected hurdle during the purchase of their home when strikes by two major unions in the industry coincided with the requirement to open an escrow account as part of the terms for transferring ownership of the property. "As soon as he opened up escrow, the WGA and SAG-AFTRA went on strike," Nash said, illustrating how unexpected financial predicaments befall families with limited wealth. The strikes threatened not only the family's immediate financial stability but also their homeownership dreams, introducing "a gap of employment that I now have to explain away," as the father put it, during a crucial phase in the loan approval process.

Amid this turmoil, signs of the family's resilience and adaptability were evident in their two-bedroom apartment. "The mother had converted a linen closet into a desk for one of the kids," showing a creative approach to their spatial constraints. This inventiveness was repeated in various nooks and crannies, which were transformed into functional spaces for study and storage, revealing a family making the best of their circumstances while aspiring for more.

"We came in and helped with the shortage," Nash said. The Homeownership Council of America was able to assist the Smiths with their sudden need, as it does with similar families, to bridge financial gaps. This approach is rooted in a particular commitment. "We don't want to see borrowers start off at a disadvantage," Nash said. His dedication to helping families in this way comes from his broader grasp of wealth inequality: "When I looked at housing data, I see hundreds of thousands of Smiths."

Data from 2020 highlights the urgency of such programs, showing that 16.1 percent of mortgage applications were declined nationwide. Alarmingly, Black applicants faced the highest denial rate at 27.1 percent, in stark contrast to white applicants, who experienced the lowest at 13.6 percent.[21] Meanwhile, the projected growth in households from 2020 to 2040—an expected net increase of 16.1 million—will be driven primarily by people of color, according to an Urban Institute analysis.[22] Hispanic households are projected to increase by 8.6 million, those of other races (predominantly Asian) by 4.8 million, and Black households by 3.4 million. In contrast, white households are anticipated to decrease by 0.6 million.

Given these projections, financial institutions stand to benefit greatly from tapping into Black, Hispanic, and Asian consumers, and SPCPs can help lenders, who are trying to make a profit, aside from the good they can provide. Nash wants lenders to see the financial benefit in creating new pathways to homeownership. "The bottom-line impact is, how much money can we make off of this?" as Nash framed the business incentive, emphasizing the need to present the narrative in a way that appeals to the financial sector's profit motive while achieving social justice outcomes.

With the Homeownership Council's intervention, the Smiths were able to move to a four-bedroom home. As Nash facilitated this transition, he captured a moment of idyllic triumph—the family standing in front of their new house, an image he fondly compares to "one of those pictures you see on a Sunday morning church fan." Getting the Smiths to closing is more than a personal victory for Nash. It is a testament to the power of targeted assistance and advocacy in overcoming barriers to homeownership.

*   *   *

WHILE SPCPs CAN be very helpful, the $5,000–$20,000 assistance they provide is nowhere near sufficient to offset the racial wealth gap or cover the down payments people need in many locations. In 2021, Black households faced the greatest likelihood of either possessing no wealth or having negative net worth, with 24 percent falling into this category, according to a 2023 Pew Research analysis.[23] White and Asian households exhibited the lowest likelihood of having no wealth or having negative net worth in 2021, with figures standing at 9 percent and 7 percent, respectively.

Hannah Jones, an economic data analyst at Realtor.com, reports that in the second quarter of 2023 the national average down payment for buying a house was 14.4 percent of the purchase price, equal to a median amount of $34,248. During this period, Louisiana saw the lowest average down payment at 9.2 percent, or $6,729, indicative of the state's more accessible housing market (notwithstanding the rising insurance costs due to climate change). At the other end, Washington, DC, had the highest average down payment rate of 20.4 percent, or a median sum of $100,800.[24]

This obstacle is added to escalating property prices and dwindling housing stock.[25] According to a 2022 National Association of Realtors (NAR) report, the availability of affordable homes for sale across the country for households earning between $75,000 and $100,000 has declined since early 2020 and the start of the pandemic, with only 245,300 homes available in December 2021, compared to 656,200 in December 2019. This translates to just one affordable listing for every sixty-five households in that income bracket, a stark drop from the one to twenty-four ratio of two years prior. These constraints inflame the racial home-ownership gap. "Nationwide, 35% of White households and only 20% of Black households have incomes greater than $100,000," according to the NAR. "Approximately

half of all homes currently listed for sale (51%) are affordable to households with at least $100,000 income and sub-
stantial variances in affordability exist by metro area."

Creating new inventory and improving affordability
is part of the mission of Parity Homes, which buys abandoned properties to forge pathways for residents to transition into ownership. With the goal of giving people more
of a stake in their own neighborhood, Parity taps into
existing groups of friends, extended family, colleagues, and
congregations in the Baltimore neighborhood of Harlem
Park and across the city to help these organic groups to buy
homes together, on a block-by-block basis.

"We use collective economics to reduce any one individual's risk, while deepening the human bonds that make
community," says Bree Jones, Parity's founder and executive
director. "If we have thirty homeowners who all move onto
a block at one time, that radically changes the dynamic of
a distressed area."

Jones has taken on the daunting challenge of addressing Baltimore's staggering number of vacant buildings. The
Abell Foundation found that Baltimore has nearly fifteen
thousand homes marked by vacant building notices, with
the vast majority—about 90 percent—situated in neighborhoods plagued by high vacancy rates and poverty.[26]
These derelict properties are a source of instability, affecting
the real estate market and the communities around them,
and fueling ongoing disinvestment and population decline.

The financial impact on the city is significant: over
$200 million, every year, in lost revenue and direct costs.
According to the foundation's report, tackling Baltimore's
vacant housing would necessitate $2.5 billion in public

investment over the next twenty years. However, this substantial public expenditure could potentially draw in $4.4
billion in private capital, offering an avenue to revitalize
these areas. Jones underscored the complexity of the issue,
noting that nearly every vacant property that has not been
seized by the city has a separate owner. With the city owning only around three thousand buildings, she emphasized
the meticulous process required to acquire and repurpose
these neglected properties.

Parity's model works across four key areas in neighborhoods with hypervacancy. First, it uses a "systems change"
approach, addressing systemic barriers that make acquisition
and redevelopment of abandoned buildings cumbersome.
Liens on property are often held by individuals, investment
groups, and speculators from outside the state who simply
walk away from these debts, neglecting the property and
piling up even more tax debt. This makes it even harder and
more expensive to resolve ownership issues. Parity works with
the city to hold absent landlords and owners accountable
and seize their property.

Second, Parity seeks to restore the social fabric of neighborhoods through collective power building and trauma-
informed healing. Parity doesn't work with individuals or
even a collection of individuals but with a community,
leveraging its interconnectedness. If racism affects people
in a collective manner, so should the repair of that harm.
Third, the model aims to alleviate the departure of longtime
residents by engaging in mutual aid. This involves collabo-
rating with the community to establish networks offering
care and support, addressing the immediate needs of neighbors.[27] Finally, Parity works through state policy to close the

gap between the appraised low value of the properties and the projected cost of restoration, making lending and construction possible.

In 2021, Jones and Parity joined forces with legislators to pass the Appraisal Gap from Historic Redlining Financial Assistance Program (H.B. 1239), a bill that established a specialized fund within the Maryland Department of Housing and Community Development. The fund aims to bridge the financial gap between the price of renovating or constructing new homes in economically challenged neighborhoods and the market value of these homes, as determined by appraisals. Designed to be distributed to developers as either grants or tax credits, the financial assistance does not exceed 35 percent of a project's construction expenses or 80 percent of the national median home sales price, depending on which is lower.

Acquiring properties and development capital are two demanding battles. Characterizing it as "hand-to-hand combat," Jones described the arduous task of identifying and locating property owners and dealing with outdated mailing addresses and disconnected phone numbers. When the owner is deceased, there are legal proceedings involved. Parity acts as its own land bank, a "public or community-owned" entity "created for a single purpose: to acquire, manage, maintain, and repurpose vacant, abandoned, and foreclosed properties—the worst abandoned houses, forgotten buildings, and empty lots."[28] Parity strategically acquires vacant properties in targeted neighborhoods, currently owning approximately forty buildings across ten blocks. It leverages the purchase of tax certificates on buildings with substantial unpaid property tax debt, sometimes reaching tens of thousands of dollars, and forecloses on these properties, securing ownership to pave the way for revitalization.

To finance these projects, Jones has to secure a variety of loans, private investments, philanthropic funding, tax credits, and other sources of funding. Operating in low-income areas poses an additional challenge, given the disparity between construction costs and local residents' purchasing power. Lenders are also hesitant to provide financing for projects that may not align with consumer demand, while investors prioritize safeguarding their returns on investment. Low-income tax credits and other public subsidies can help, but most tax incentive programs tied to affordable housing are geared toward rental properties.

Jones has found various ways to fill the gap. When she received the Johns Hopkins University Social Innovation Lab award in 2020, she invested the $25,000 award in Parity.[29] Two years later, JPMorgan Chase invested $2 million in the organization toward two hundred new homes for low-income families. The funding also supported the creation of a construction apprenticeship program. This funding was part of a larger $20 million commitment from JPMorgan Chase aimed at fostering economic equity and mobility in Baltimore.[30] Jones also joined the board of directors and leads the investment committee at Ignite Capital, a social impact fund with the mission to "empower Baltimore social enterprises in economically distressed communities by providing the financial resources to spur economic activity."[31]

Beyond acquiring and developing property, Jones works to identify the homeowners, sometimes thirty or more, who will move into a block as a group, creating up-front demand for the dwellings. This is part of Parity's innovative approach to community building, fostering organic connections among residents. By creating a "groundswell" of people with existing relationships—family members, friends, sorority members, and colleagues—Parity mitigates the risk of moving into a neighborhood undergoing transition. The built-in social fabric reduces the new homeowners' anxiety, giving them a sense of belonging even before moving in.

At the time of writing, Parity Homes had forty individuals in different stages of homeownership and was constructing five more homes, all presold to people with cultivated relationships to the community. Predominantly comprised of young professionals aged between twenty-five and thirty-eight, the collective encompasses a wide range of occupations and family arrangements. The residents include software engineers, educators affiliated with the University of Maryland, artists, and entrepreneurs, reflecting a multifaceted population. The family structures vary from single people to married couples with children and single and adoptive parents.

The shared experience of discrimination, which makes it hard for Black people to buy a home, own a business, or accrue capital, has forced Black families to pioneer collective initiatives, such as communal farming plots, Black commons, Freedom Farms, Black credit unions, mutual aid networks, and community land trusts.[32] Beyond ownership, these enterprises emphasize community self-sufficiency, grassroots-led development, and the redistribution of power from oppressive structures.

In their analysis, scholars Tracy Hadden Loh and Hanna Love from the Brookings Institution identified a range of community ownership models, including limited equity co-ops, in which residents buy shares in a development instead of individual units, committing to resell their shares at a set price to maintain long-term affordability.[33] Common-interest communities share ownership of assets such as roofs and heating systems. Cooperatives involve joint ownership by consumers, workers, or residents who contribute capital through membership fees. Neighborhood real estate investment trusts (REITs) enable both mission-driven investors and residents to invest in large-scale, income-generating real estate. Community investment trusts offer a low-cost, risk-protected avenue for residents to accumulate equity in commercial properties. There are a few hundred of each of these models around the country, a far cry from the demand and need.

Jones's work has not been without challenges. She has faced pushback from some quarters, with concerns about the demographics of Parity homeowners and gentrification.

"We recognized what happened in DC. We recognized what happened in Harlem and Brooklyn, New York," she said, referring to the displacement of longtime residents by more monied newcomers. "We're really trying to figure out how we can prevent that from happening again in predominantly Black neighborhoods," she acknowledged. "But we want to be part of revitalization and restoration, and we want to do it in equitable ways that keep legacy residents housed and centered."

* * *

COLLEGE-EDUCATED AND HAVING worked on Wall Street, Jones initially encountered skepticism about her ability to make a meaningful impact in West Baltimore. However, she argued that the financial vulnerability of many Black Americans transcends educational attainment, pointing to the economic fragility and the thin line that separates low- and middle-income status. The reality of being Black in America, Jones said, "is that we're all like one missed paycheck away from being kind of in financial crisis." She noted, "Middle-class Black folks still have less wealth than white high school dropouts."

As well as providing homeownership opportunities, Parity supports residents through initiatives focused on property maintenance, tax assistance, and estate issues. "We try to think about the whole spectrum of the Black experience with housing and how we can assist where possible," she said. "We're also starting to do some affordable rental housing as well because we know not everyone is ready to buy a home, but they still need affordable places to live."

"All I can do is create the opportunity," Jones concluded. "And then, if people like and open the door, and if folks walk through the door, then let's all build together."

In 2018, the National Association of Real Estate Brokers set a visionary goal to boost Black homeownership by two million within five years. Then NAREB president Jeffrey Hicks emphasized the urgent need to reverse a decades-long decline in homeownership rates. "Black homeownership is the first, and most essential step to build economic strength within our communities," said Hicks. "We've lost more ground than we've gained over the past 50 years. Whether through unmeasurable losses of equity during the country's last economic meltdown, consistently high unemployment rates, unfavorable federal and state policies restricting affordable homeownership, or systemic mortgage lending barriers, Black homeownership—and therefore our wealth-building potential as a people—remains diminished."[34]

The COVID-19 pandemic and persistent racial biases disrupted this ambitious target. In response, it is imperative to set new objectives tailored to each market. This entails implementing clear metrics to locate prospective borrowers currently renting, creating SPCPs to expand eligibility, and enhancing housing inventory to accommodate an envisioned growth in homeownership.

MARRIAGE MATERIAL

My son Roby could barely move when I attempted to wake him for school one mild spring morning. He rarely got out of bed on my first attempt, but this time I could immediately tell something was different. He had the kind of look that a parent knows can't be faked. As we were still officially in a pandemic, my immediate suspicion was COVID.

As I extended my hand to his forehead to check his temperature, I could feel the heat rising from his visibly aching body. My touch confirmed the fever but I took his temperature to make sure. It was 103 degrees. Not quite in a panic, I still knew I had to take him to the emergency room. A tall twelve-year-old, he could now barely sit up on his own. Roby was wearing the sweatpants he'd had on the day before, but I grabbed a sweatshirt and put it on him like I used to when he was too young to dress himself. I pushed his limp arms through the sleeves, cringing from the heat every time our skin touched.

Roby usually argued against even the suggestion of

going to see a doctor; now he wanted relief too much to put up a fight.

The hospital was about twenty minutes away, but my anxiety about his obvious suffering made it seem much farther. He pressed his head against the cool glass window to relieve the pain, keeping his eyes tightly shut. I tried to focus on the road, not to keep from crashing but to distract myself from the fear of what was wrong with my child.

We gingerly walked to the emergency room and were checked in. After we'd answered some questions and Roby was swabbed to test for COVID, he fell asleep.

I sat with him, in what felt like a nightmare. Every parent dreads the waiting beside their ailing child lying on a hospital bed. For most of my adult life, I'd felt a sense of control or at least that I had some influence over a potential outcome. Now the power was in someone else's hands. I'm not religious, but I prayed hard—for him, for the hospital staff, and for myself to keep me from thinking the worst.

After more than an hour, a physician came and confirmed that Roby had indeed contracted COVID. She calmed my fears by charting a straightforward path to recovery and Roby's eyes cracked open at the news that he would be okay.

Both Roby and I held chests full of ease on the drive back home.

Roby went straight to his bed and I dragged myself across the hallway to my room. Emotionally exhausted, I sat upright against the headboard, contemplating how much Roby meant to me. As a crack of light crept through the blackout curtains, I said out loud, "Being a single mother is hard."

* * *

ACCORDING TO MY research at the Brookings Institution, the percentage of Black children not living with their fathers is negatively correlated with life expectancy. In the average county in our sample, 57 percent of Black children did not live with their fathers, according to Census Bureau data.

To be clear, when Black fathers control their children's living arrangements, they spend at least as much time playing, reading, helping with homework, and doing other activities with their offspring as do non-Hispanic white fathers. However, because Black fathers are more than twice as likely as non-Hispanic white fathers to live apart from their children, the overall effect is one of less involvement.

My son not only lives with his father—I am also the primary custodial parent. For twelve years, Roby had resided under the same roof as both his parents, but after a sudden unraveling, I gained full custody. Putting myself in a single mother's shoes was something of a reckoning with my family's new reality, which gave me insight into why children living apart from their fathers, rather than with their mothers, is one of the strongest negative predictors of life expectancy. Where health outcomes are concerned, resources matter, with wealth being one of the strongest factors.

"It all starts at home" is a something we say, believing that the family is the foundation for success. But the phrase is misleading, overlooking the evidence that material resources, including the home itself, shape the futures of the people living in it. A more empirically grounded version might be, "It all starts with owning a home," for example.

Clearly, rearing children requires material and other less tangible support, which can be enhanced by cohabitation, marriage, or any dedicated partnership. It makes sense to assume that two incomes in one household yield more wealth than two incomes in two separate homes, and the more wealth that a family has, of which income is a part, the healthier it is likely to be. This is one reason why children of two-parent households outperform their single-parent peers in education, health, and income over time.

Yes, resources matter. However, in the American context, not only race but also gender influences the kinds and extent of a family's resources. In a patriarchal society, policy privileges and empowers maleness in many ways, to the extent that the privileges of being male can represent a whole family, covering for the contributions of a female partner. Men on average receive higher pay. Job positions that are traditionally assigned to women like teaching receive lower compensation. Tax policy has traditionally revolved around men's economic status. Thus there can be a resource penalty in a patriarchal society when a child doesn't live with a father.

For Black families, economic power is diminished further by the intersection of racism and sexism. On average, Black men make less than white men, and Black women earn less than both white and Black men. Michelle Holder, past president and CEO of the Washington Center for Equitable Growth, called the effect on Black women of racial and gender disparities the "double gap."[1]

The historical policies that prohibited Black wealth

creation and growth were enhanced by policies that prohibited Black marriage. Prior to the Thirteenth Amendment,
Black people were considered property, so they neither
marry nor create wealth, instead being the assets that generated wealth for white Americans. The Civil Rights Act
of 1866 codified the rights of free people to own, sell, or
lease personal and real property, and to enter into contracts, including marriage. In most states it was illegal for
Black people to marry a white partner until 1967 when
the Supreme Court in *Loving v. Virginia* struck down laws
banning interracial marriage. These factors undoubtedly
resulted in deviations from the idealized nuclear family,
but the divergent marriage rates between Black and white
people also reflect a different economic and social reality.

The median age at first marriage has increased for
both men and women in the United States over the past
fifty years. In 1970, men typically married at 23.2 years,
while women married at 20.8 years. By 2020, these ages
had risen to 30.5 years for men and 28.1 years for women,
according to a 2022 Census report.[2] The percentage of
never-married men in 1970 was 28.1 percent, compared
to 22.1 percent of women across all groups. By 2020, these
figures had risen to 35.8 percent for men and 30.0 percent
for women. However, among Black people, the percentage
of those who had never married was higher in 1970: 35.6
percent of men and 27.7 percent of women. By 2020, these
percentages had increased significantly, to 51.4 percent for
Black men and 47.5 percent for Black women never having
been married.

Black people have largely pursued a nuclear family
structure,[3] striving to look like the Cosbys in *The Cosby*

Show. However, the racism and sexism of labor markets and the criminal justice system, in particular, have made creating that archetype less achievable. In his book *The Truly Disadvantaged,* sociologist William Julius Wilson introduced the concept of the "marriageable male," that is, a man who could contribute to the household income. He suggested that limited economic prospects for Black men and high rates of incarceration were responsible for declining marriage rates and the increase in Black woman-headed households.

The disparities in marriage rates could be attributed to a mismatch between, on the one hand, access to employment, housing, and educational opportunities and, on the other, the economic standards of marriageability.[4] Indeed, many studies examining delays in marriage have focused on income, broadly finding that people with higher incomes marry earlier.[5] Education shows a similar trajectory, as more-educated Black people have higher rates of marriage. Overall, wealth is a strong positive predictor of marriage—the greater a person's wealth, the more likely it is that they will be married.[6] Wealth enables possession of a home, a car, and health care, all the necessities of supporting a family.[7]

Although income and education are key factors in marriage, looking at it through this lens tends to encourage seeing cohabition as a matter of individual choice. In this view, Black men and women just need to make better personal and relationship decisions if they want better health and financial outcomes and to gain more power as a by-product of marriage. Conservatives and liberals alike have taken this position while overlooking the policies and practices that limit economic opportunities.

Conversations about marriage should focus on the role of wealth as a *precondition*. Currently, we are distracted from acknowledging and acting on this precondition by a persistent narrative that marriage is a solution to poverty and that the lack of it causes poverty. Yes, there are economic benefits to marriage, but a skewed focus on it as the main driver of positive outcomes diverts attention from eliminating the discrimination that extracts wealth and makes marriage less likely. Worse, seeing marriage as a remedy for community ills shifts the blame away from the discriminatory policies that inhibit growth and lays it at the feet of Black people.

* * *

IN A 2011 study that examined wealth as a predictor of marriage, Harvard University researcher Daniel Schneider found that men and women who enter marriage are more likely to possess vehicles, homes, and bank accounts compared to those who remain unmarried. Surprisingly, the study found that women who own their own homes appear to be less likely to marry.

Schneider inserted race in his model to see if the gap in asset ownership or wealth helps explain the racial marriage gap and he found that it is a significant factor. For men in his study, he saw that about half of those who were unmarried at age twenty had married by twenty-seven if they owned assets, compared to only one-quarter who had never owned assets. Additionally, assets increased the likelihood of marriage by age forty-six, to about 80 percent, compared to 40 percent of those who had never owned any.

When Schneider attended to wealth when looking at

a Black man and woman entering their first marriage, the gap was narrowed by about 30 percent and 36 percent respectively.

Wealth doesn't just improve the likelihood of marriage, it also helps sustain marriage. In a 2016 study published in the *Journal of the Social Sciences*, Cornell University researchers Alicia Eads and Laura Tach examined its role in the dissolution of cohabitations.[8] The researchers defined family structure as adults residing together in the same household, and they identified marital or cohabitation dissolution as a change in the household family composition, indicating separation, legal divorce, or one cohabiting partner no longer dwelling in the same home. Wealth was assessed using four components: secured debt (primarily mortgages), unsecured debt (such as credit card balances), liquid assets (savings and checking accounts), and illiquid assets (car and property values). The study also explored racial differences between couples.

Before looking at the impact of wealth, Eads and Tach found that Black couples are 53 percent more likely than white ones to end their relationships. Accounting for economic factors such as income, employment, and education decreases this gap, with Black couples being 41 percent more likely to split. When the researchers introduced assets and debts, the likelihood of breaking up for Black couples fell to 29 percent. This suggests that assets and debts have a significant effect on stabilizing relationships, cutting the gap between Black and white couples by about 45 percent.

There are benefits to wealth creation *after* marriage, too, particularly for Black people. According to a 2021 analysis by W. Bradford Wilcox, married Americans possess over double the average assets of divorced and never-married individuals, even when adjusting for gender, age, education, race, and ethnicity.[9] On average, men and women in stable marriages have assets exceeding $640,000, while those who have remarried possess assets surpassing $450,000. In contrast, Wilcox found that those who are divorced or have never married typically have only around $167,000 in assets by the time they reach preretirement age. Married couples save more, taking advantage of economies of scale.

Differences in wealth based on family structure extend to both white and Black Americans, albeit not in the same way. Wilcox found that married white Americans exhibit more than double the wealth (approximately $750,000) of their unmarried counterparts (approximately $300,000). The impact of marital status is even more pronounced for Black people, with married individuals having over three times the wealth of their unmarried peers, totaling about $230,000 versus $65,000. Marriage alone does not resolve the racial gap, however, given that the average wealth of married Black Americans is lower than that of white married people.

There exists a chicken-and-egg dynamic in that past policies prohibited both marriage and wealth creation. But to what extent do racial differences in marital histories account for disparities in wealth? This was the primary question of researchers Fenaba R. Addo of University of North Carolina and Daniel T. Lichter of Cornell University in a 2013 study published in the *Journal of Marriage and Family*.[10] Addo and Lichter focused on wealth and asset accumulation among Black women aged fifty-one to sixty-one, born between 1931 and 1953, looking at housing, stocks, checking and savings accounts, vehicles, and savings. The data was compared with that of white women of the same age.

They found that nearly 68 percent were currently married, with a significant racial disparity: only 37 percent of the Black women were married compared to 72 percent of the white women. Among the unmarried women, 28 percent had some union history, with Black women overrepresented in the never-married category at 11.5 percent compared to 3.2 percent. Additionally, of the married women, 51 percent had been continuously coupled with no disruptions, while 14 percent had remarried after divorce, and nearly 2 percent as widows. Statistically significant differences were found between Black and white women in categories such as separated, divorced, and widowed. Further analysis showed that Black women married on average one year later than white women and had an average of seven fewer years in marriage over their lifetimes.

Despite controlling for other factors, like employment and health, the researchers also saw meaningful wealth disparities between the women in the sample, with Black women having substantially lower total and nonhousing wealth. For instance, at the 25th percentile (meaning the least-wealthy quarter), Black women had zero nonhousing wealth compared to $15,000 for white women. The gap persisted across all quantiles of wealth distribution, with Black women consistently having less. Additionally, being unmarried, especially never married, was associated with lower wealth accumulation across the wealth distribution.

*   *   *

TAX POLICY, DESIGNED to reflect the lived experiences of white Americans, has penalized Black people for their family dynamics. Dorothy A. Brown, in her book *The Whiteness of Wealth*, elucidates how the history of tax subsidies for marriage disproportionately benefited white families. Notably, the development of the joint tax return, assumed to benefit all Americans equally, arose from the advocacy of one wealthy white couple, Henry and Charlotte Seaborn, who leveraged their wealth to lobby for changes in the tax code and reduce their tax burden.

The Seaborns epitomized the supposedly ideal nuclear family, with Henry serving as the breadwinner—a vice president of a shipbuilding company—and Charlotte working in the home, reflecting the single-income model that described 85 percent of white married households in the late 1940s. Together, they successfully sued the IRS and persuaded Congress to enact laws allowing them to split Henry's income with Charlotte, deducting half of the married exemption from each. The Seaborns' maneuver effectively divided their tax burden, placing them in lower tax brackets individually. Previously, individuals without income were not required to file a tax return, leaving most Black Americans exempt due to low income thresholds.

This shift initiated a cascade of marriage bonuses and penalties that favored taxation of couples rather than individual spouses. Within a progressive income tax system, a couple's combined income may face higher or lower taxation than the incomes of two single individuals, and this has benefited white, wealthier families. While couples are not obliged to file jointly, opting for separate returns typically leads to increased tax liability.[11] When the new system was created, Black people found themselves facing more penalties, exacerbating financial strain. Additionally, Black families lived in predominantly dual-income households, which disadvantaged them further, as their combined wages frequently placed them in a higher tax bracket. More broadly, systemic efforts to encourage marriage effectively discriminated against single individuals, disproportionately penalizing Black people who were more likely than their white counterparts to be single.

Power building is a collective endeavor, and marriage and family embody perhaps the ultimate collective commitment. Accordingly any conversation about marriage rates and the associated benefits must be contextualized within a framework of past and present-day racism and sexism, which have deprived Black men and women of the wealth crucial for supporting families and diminished the likelihood that they will get married in the first place. It is impossible to improve marriage rates without addressing the policies that make marriage less likely and less advantageous for Black people.

* * *

ACADEMIC AND POPULAR discourse about Black marriage or the lack thereof is littered with baseless assumptions about the interpersonal proclivities or dysfunction of Black men and women. Vapid texts like *Act Like a Lady, Think Like a Man* by comedian and talk-show host Steve Harvey typify the narrative (the book was even adapted into a movie), arguing that if we could only read and adjust Black attitudes, marriage rates would naturally rise.

It is also flawed logic to treat marriage as purely a

mathematical construct, commodifying accomplishments and physical characteristics. The late Kevin Samuels, a prominent online Black image consultant, popularized the phrase *high-value man* to express elevated worth in the marriage marketplace based on income, education, and physical characteristics like height. Samuels often pointed to a mismatch between a woman's perceived value (typically higher than her real value in the market) and the value of the man she thinks she deserves. Putting Black people on a virtual auction block for marriage is to miss the fundamental causes of low marriage rates.

Blaming people instead of policy is also common in the current intraracial discourse. Rather than looking at the causes for the mismatch between access to employment and economic standards of marriageability, women and men accuse each other of not being ready for commitment. As for policymakers, who are ostensibly charged with creating or removing legislation to influence behaviors, they often have as much credibility as comedians when it comes to their views on the declining rates of Black marriage. Yet they have played the blame game at every level of government through policy statements, speeches, and directives, which have persistently framed Black singlehood as a function of maladaptive choices, void of political context.

One federal statement stands out for its detrimental influence in placing responsibility directly on Black people: the 1965 report *The Negro Family: The Case for National Action*, or the Moynihan Report, published by the Office of Policy Planning and Research of the US Department of Labor. The report does point to slavery and discrimination as causal factors in many of the outcomes it aimed to address, but it also accepts the inherent inequality of a patriarchal society while not so subtly laying blame for the state of the Black family at the feet of women. In the chapter "The Tangle of Pathology," the authors wrote, "In essence, the Negro community has been forced into a matriarchal structure which, because it is so out of line with the rest of the American society, seriously retards the progress of the group as a whole, and imposes a crushing burden on the Negro male and, in consequence, on a great many Negro women as well."

The Moynihan Report perpetuates the notion that Black men and women must conform to societal norms while overlooking the myriad forces that either facilitated or hindered marriage: the housing policies that failed to insure mortgages in Black neighborhoods; redlining; the exclusion of Black people from the GI Bill of 1944, with its education and housing opportunities; and segregation, which restricted access to quality education, employment, and housing. One can only speculate on the extent to which these discriminatory practices robbed Black families of the wealth to enter into and stabilize marriage.

Another enduring consequence of the report's framing of the Black family as pathological is that it invited legislators to enact punitive policies, which were completely at odds with promoting human development, let alone marriage. Beginning in the 1980s, the War on Drugs targeted Black and Latino men, leading to increased incarceration rates, which removed potential partners from communities and diminished their viability as suitable mates.

Brookings Institution scholar Adam Looney and Nicholas Turner of the Federal Reserve Board examined a population of approximately 2.9 million individuals, drawn from administrative prisoner records submitted annually by the Federal Bureau of Prisons and state prison agencies to the IRS starting in 2012.[12] They matched these records with earnings and tax filing data spanning from 1999 to 2014, offering insights into pre- and post-incarceration employment, earnings, and select demographic details. Additionally, for a subset of 497,000 incarcerated people born between 1980 and 1986, the study included information about their childhood neighborhoods, as well as their parents' income and marital status.

Looney and Turner found that within the first year after their release, only 55 percent of former prisoners reported any earnings, and the median annual income among those employed was $10,090. Merely 20 percent earned above $15,000, the federal minimum wage for full-time work. Despite their eligibility for tax incentives targeting low-income workers, including ex-felons, ex-prisoners struggle to secure stable employment. Interestingly, their difficulties in the labor market tend to predate their incarceration, with only 49 percent of prime-age men employed three years prior to imprisonment, earning an annual median of $6,250. These continuity-in-employment challenges suggest that while incarceration may affect earnings (and marriageability), the root causes of labor market struggles for ex-prisoners likely preceded their time in prison, restricting economic growth and human development.

Considering the adverse outcomes for children of imprisoned adults, perhaps even more unnerving is that mass incarceration and racially biased policing hinder wealth accumulation for multiple generations. Incarceration, particularly when done in a manner that doesn't rehabilitate, literally arrests wealth development, removing men from their communities, and perpetuating a cycle of poverty.

Blaming people rather than policy doesn't just skew relations, it encourages a toxic intra-racial discourse that can veer into what could be called "oppression Olympics" — a competition for the title of most oppressed. Black women face a double gap. Black men are incarcerated at rates that take out potential partners. Underresourced schools, housing discrimination, and lack of access to capital limit Black men's and women's potential—collectively. The effect is evident in distinct outcomes across gender lines and a distinct gendered discourse around responsibility for confronting these systems based on whose suffering is greatest: Black women are in charge of reproductive rights and Black men carry the burden of changing prison systems.

Racism and sexism are tightly braided systems that collectively affect Black men and women. Marriage rate is one of many indicators revealing the effect of these systems on Black communities. Marriage can help people cope with the financial losses stemming from racism and sexism, but it should never be seen as a panacea for white supremacy. Black people are not going marry away these ills.

From a policy perspective, marriage has historically supported the advancement of the white nuclear family and white men's wealth. Along with everyone else, it is in Black people's interest to deconstruct systems of inequality. Therefore, we should not endorse Black participation in marriage as a foundational problem to be solved. Racism and sexism are the problems to be solved, and Black people's collective work to dismantle these systems will do more to elevate authentic unions of love.

Black women and men share a fate determined by our collective ability to restore the wealth that has been extracted from our community. Certainly, we should understand the economic benefits of marriage, but first we must recognize wealth as its precondition.

As for the action that Black people can take to improve their outcomes and increase the likelihood of marriage, a family that protests racial and gender inequality together stays together. Removing the barriers to equality is not only political; it's romantic. Love is a given in relationships. Love is not in short supply. However, love realized in marriage should be viewed as a by-product of social justice.

THE COMMUNITY AS
A GOOD SCHOOL

"In the twenty-first century, our children have one of three options: take something, break something, or make something," New Orleans native Calvin Mackie, engineer and founder of the nonprofit STEM NOLA, told me. STEM NOLA conducts hands-on science projects out of school on the weekends. Calvin Mackie's observation highlights an undeniable truth: without access to quality education and the acquisition of valuable skills, young people are left with limited and often detrimental choices.

This stark reality is underscored by statistics from Louisiana, where nearly half (48 percent) of the incarcerated population entered the prison system without a high school diploma or its equivalent, according to the Louisiana Department of Public Safety and Corrections website.[1] The Prison Policy Initiative, a nonprofit, nonpartisan research organization focused on mass criminalization, did a comprehensive analysis of where prisoners came from as well as local jail rates.[2] PPI found that in New Orleans, where

Black individuals constitute 58 percent of the population, they represent 74 percent of the arrests made by local police.

The pattern repeats in the state's other large centers, which are majority Black. These disparities in arrest rates resonate in Louisiana's prison demographics: while only 33 percent of the overall population is Black, Black people make up 65 percent of incarcerated people.

During the 2021–22 academic year, Louisiana's auditor's office gathered data on the state's K–12 school population of an estimated 775,583 students. The demographic breakdown was approximately 48 percent white, 37.8 percent Black, 8.6 percent Hispanic, and 5.6 percent other racial minorities.[3] The audit unveiled that 71 percent of students in public schools are classified as economically disadvantaged, revealing a negative correlation between a school's rate of children in the category and its academic performance.

Reflecting on these findings, Jan Moller, executive director of the Louisiana Budget Project, noted that the auditor's analysis corroborates a well-documented reality. "The biggest indicator of a school's performance is poverty, and we've known that," said Moller. "Poverty and school performance are inextricably linked."[4]

* * *

WE SAY THAT knowledge is power, and one can interpret the phrase to refer to the impact of information and education on human development and liberty. The knowledge gained through education endows people with the skills and wherewithal to optimize their health, employment, well-being, and safety. Higher levels of education are strongly linked to behaviors that contribute to robust communities, increasing participation in civic activities such as voting and volunteering, and decreasing the probability of criminal behavior.[5]

Despite making up only 14.4 percent of the US population, Black Americans account for more than one-third of the prison population.[6] This disparity is largely influenced by a criminal justice system rife with anti-Black bias and racial prejudice. Additionally, individuals who are undereducated and underachieving are particularly susceptible to falling into this system. The statistics are stark: one in three Black men without a high school diploma or GED is likely to face incarceration, in sharp contrast to one in eight white men. The consequences of incarceration extend beyond the individual, notably affecting their children.[7] Regardless of other socioeconomic factors, children with incarcerated parents face heightened risks of dropping out of school, developing learning disabilities such as ADHD, engaging in disruptive behavior in the classroom, and experiencing health issues ranging from migraines and asthma to depression and anxiety, and even enduring homelessness.

The communal price for the lack of access to education has made its pursuit by Black people across generations a mission with a purpose that extends beyond the benefits to the individual. Historical Black power movements acknowledged that education is fundamentally tied to people's collective status as citizens of this country. Adequate education is seen as a prerequisite for full citizenship, empowering individuals to assert their identity and participate in democracy, essentially an outgrowth of emancipation.

Abolitionist, statesman, and civil rights leader Frederick Douglass highlighted the role of education in breaking the chains of servitude. "Once you learn to read, you will be forever free," he wrote, asserting the liberating power of literacy. In his autobiography, *Narrative of the Life of Frederick Douglass, an American Slave*, Douglass quoted his owner: "If you teach that nigger (speaking of myself) how to read, there would be no keeping him. It would forever unfit him to be a slave." In today's context, we could replace "slave" with "inmate."

The essence of knowledge's power lies in its permanency—aside from life and mental illness, knowledge is one of the most challenging assets to strip from a person. While essential material and social possessions—money, homes, voting rights, memberships, and degrees—can and have been taken away, knowledge gives people the ability to rebuild and prevent future efforts to deprive them of basic liberties and personal goods.

One form of education has been elemental in the historic Black pursuit of power: cultural literacy and knowledge of self. Scholars and activists Kwame Ture and Charles V. Hamilton, in their book *Black Power: The Politics of Liberation*, articulated the need "to struggle for the right to create our own terms through which to define ourselves and our relationship to society, and to have these terms recognized." Slavery, Jim Crow racism, and decades of discrimination provide a strong rationale for this aim of education. To justify the denial of membership, wealth, and opportunity, society needed to deem Black people and their communities as unworthy or unfit for essential investment, rights, and privileges. Ture, Hamilton, and other proponents of Black power recognized the importance of schools as essential sites where Black communities could systematically engage in self-definition and actively dismantle or unlearn the narratives of white supremacy.

For improving life outcomes, gaining knowledge of self, and uplifting society, education and good schooling are essential components of Black power.

* * *

FINDINGS FROM THE Black Progress Index underscore that education, measured by higher attainment rates and school exam performance, has a positive effect on life expectancy. In counties where Black adults aged twenty-five and over possess at least a bachelor's degree, there is an additional 0.38 years of life expectancy for every standard increase in this educational level. Similarly, life expectancy increases by 0.45 years for every standard increase in the percentage of Black students scoring at or above proficiency in statewide math exams.

As we have seen, there is a strong correlation between income, education, and health, regardless of racial group. Educated people are more likely to be aware of, embrace, and maintain healthy practices, such as abstaining from smoking, limiting alcohol consumption, avoiding high-carb diets, and remaining active. If they have higher income levels, they will also have greater access to resources such as nutritious food, exercise, stress-reducing services, and quality health care.[8] Residing near higher-educated, wealthier individuals further enhances health through improvements in markets, safety, and government policies and resources.[9]

However, the power of education has its limits. Education is not the great equalizer. At all educational levels, its financial benefits for Hispanic and African Americans tend to be less pronounced than they are for non-Hispanic white and Asian Americans. While family wealth typically rises with educational achievement in the United States, there are notable distinctions, based on race and ethnicity, in its influence on wealth accumulation. Specifically, higher educational attainment more often results in comparatively smaller gains for Hispanic and Black families. In a 2016 study by William Emmons and Lowell Ricketts,[10] they noted that the anticipated income gaps between Hispanic and Black high school graduates and their white peers were $5 and $14 per hour, respectively. That gap rose to $19 and $21 for college graduates, with a further increase to $30 and $56 for postgraduate families.

The cycle of economic deficit, educational disadvantage, and heightened incarceration risk shows how deeply education is intertwined with issues of justice and equality, highlighting the importance of providing educational opportunities as a means of increasing wealth, building Black power, and breaking the cycle of incarceration. The National Assessment of Educational Progress, known as the "Nation's Report Card," shows there are significant disparities to address. Data from 2022 for fourth-grade mathematics reveals a proficiency level among Black students of 15 percent.[11] This is in decline from the previous assessment in 2019, when the percentage stood at 20 percent. However, only 1 percent of Black students performed at proficient levels in 1990, showing there has been considerable growth over a relatively short period. Among Black eighth graders, 9 percent performed at or above proficient levels in math, a decrease from the 14 percent recorded in 2019. (It should be noted that most researchers and educators attribute the decline to the pandemic as there was a drop during the same period among all racial groups.)

On the reading portion of the NAEP, 17 percent of Black students performed at or above proficient levels in 2022, showing a 1 percent decrease since 2019. However, according to data from 1992, only 8 percent of Black students achieved proficiency. On eighth-grade reading, 16 percent of Black students performed at or above proficient levels in 2022, a slight increase over the 15 percent recorded in 2019. Comparatively, the data from 1992 shows that 9 percent of Black students were proficient.

In addition to indicators of future performance, standardized tests are good proxies for the wealth into which students were born. Income and other wealth factors track with test performance, with a student's score correlating with their parents' income, according to College Board data. Similarly, the less money parents make, the more likely it is that their children are denied a chance at a selective institution.[12] The educational divide between rich and the poor has widened slightly, with the gap in scores between those who make less and more than $80,000 a year having increased from 2012 to 2016, according to a 2016 ACT report.[13] This means that initiatives to improve education and increase literary and numeracy should go hand in hand with building wealth and income, decreasing debt, and endeavors to enhance community prosperity, issues that go beyond the schoolhouse. Conversely, any efforts to suppress Black people's educational opportunities must be recognized as an attack on Black wealth, autonomy, and empowerment. The need to enhance academic performance and boost college attendance rates is a given, but how to accomplish this is a burning question. In recent times, this debate has been focused on the contentious issues of standards-based testing and accountability, charter schools, school vouchers, and school takeovers. Although narrowly concerned with academic outcomes, these initiatives also affect the allocation of resources to school-district boundaries, the selection of contractors, recruitment of teachers, and choices of curricular content. Such decisions are deeply connected to wealth generation for individuals and communities. Efforts to cancel student debt and create free college also belong on a Black power agenda, since college attainment tracks with wealth. These decisions and policies are deeply connected to wealth generation and are inherently political, dictating the use of the resources that foreshadow academic success.

* * *

CONTEXTUALIZING KNOWLEDGE FOR Black people in the United States involves recognizing the historic struggles of former African slaves for universal education in the South. In James D. Anderson's seminal work *The Education of Blacks in the South, 1860–1935*, he provides insight into the central aims of Black education, emphasizing that the quest for learning was a means for African Americans to assert their self-determination and foster literate, cultural communities. During Reconstruction, to achieve this goal numerous schools were established by philanthropic organizations, missionary groups, and government agencies such as the Freedmen's Bureau. In tandem with external efforts to provide education, the existence of "native schools" run by ex-slaves highlights the intrinsic value placed on learning within the Black community.

However, the struggles of Black people to gain access to learning has been matched by the efforts to restrict it. Between 1740 and 1867, anti-literacy laws in the United States banned both enslaved and, in certain instances, free Black Americans from acquiring reading and writing skills, ostensibly to discourage escapes, revolts, and the exchange of knowledge and ideas among the enslaved.[14] Following the abolition of slavery, Jim Crow laws enforced racial segregation in public facilities, including schools, throughout the former Confederate states. The Supreme Court legitimized segregation practices under the doctrine of "separate but equal," cementing this in law until the landmark 1954 ruling in *Brown v. Board of Education of Topeka*, which declared state-sanctioned segregation in public schools a violation of the Fourteenth Amendment. Yet that ruling did not stop the efforts to prevent the education of Black children. Many southern states fought mightily to thwart moves to integrate schools, which would have helped create more equitable funding systems. And a form of stealth segregation was practiced widely in the way school district boundaries were drawn, which, in turn, dictated student school assignments, thereby perpetuating divisions along racial and ethnic lines. Decades after court desegregation orders, the legacy of racial segregation still lingers. In May 2024, the Louisiana Supreme Court approved a decades-long effort to create a new, overwhelmingly white Baton Rouge–area school system, separating from the majority-Black part of the district. As reported by the nonprofit education news outlet The 74, "the secession will likely cost East Baton Rouge Parish Public Schools 10,000 students and 25% of its $700 million budget."[15] A 2019 study found eighteen of these "splinter" districts in the South that seceded from larger school districts in the years between 2000 and 2015.[16] They were all located in seven counties in Alabama, Louisiana, and Tennessee.

In the 2020–21 academic year, the Government Accountability Office reported that over a third of US students, approximately 18.5 million, were enrolled in schools where 75 percent or more of the student body shared the same race or ethnicity.[17] These findings also highlight a trend in which newly established school districts, which separated from larger existing ones, tend to have a significantly higher representation of white and Asian students compared to the districts from which they departed.

In higher education, a federal analysis spanning from 1987 to 2020 unveils a persistent pattern of underfunding for historically Black land-grant universities.[18] Out of the nineteen institutions, sixteen have faced financial shortfalls totaling $13 billion, with only Ohio and Delaware providing equitable funding. The remaining HBCUs encounter state funding disparities ranging from $172 million to $2.14 billion when compared to their predominantly white counterparts.

These and most other battles over education are power plays focused not only on the control of resources but also over who should lead a city, state, and country. Education is often a stage, frequently hidden, to wage larger political battles.

In the wake of the 2020 presidential election, after

Donald Trump lost decisively, conservative political opera-
tives scrambled to assess the damage and looked for a fresh
political platform that would energize current voters. Education came into view. Conservative lawmakers started passing
state laws to ban books and courses that espoused critical
race theory—scholarship that emerged in the 1970s identifying the systemic and legal structures of racism in American
society. The Idaho House of Representatives passed a higher
education bill stating that CRT and similar work "exacerbate
and inflame divisions on the basis of sex, race, ethnicity, religion, color, national origin, or other criteria in ways contrary
to the unity of the nation and the well-being of the state of
Idaho and its citizens."[19] Since 2021, Republican lawmakers in nearly every state, totaling forty-four nationwide, have
advanced legislation targeting educational content related
to race and racism, according to a report published in the
same year by *Education Week*.[20] The report showed that eighteen states have enacted laws to restrict critical race theory.
The GOP took further aim at "woke politics," which they
argue is taught in schools through CRT (in fact an academic
framework typically offered at colleges or graduate school).

In 2022, as part of his presidential run, Florida Republican governor Ron DeSantis promoted state legislation
known as the "Stop WOKE Act," the acronym standing
for "Wrong to Our Kids and Employees." The bill was also
called the Individual Freedom Act. The law prohibited
teaching or instruction that "espouses, promotes, advances,
inculcates, or compels" students or employees to believe
certain concepts related to race, gender and sexuality.

The following year, the Florida Board of Education
approved new standards for how Black history should be

taught in the state's public schools.[21] In the context of teaching children to analyze events that involved Africans from the nation's founding through Reconstruction, the revised curriculum requires lessons to show "how slaves developed skills which, in some instances, could be applied for their personal benefit."

The reaction to the notion that slavery developed skills as if it were a community college workforce program was swift. "How can our students ever be equipped for the future if they don't have a full, honest picture of where we've come from? Florida's students deserve a world-class education that equips them to be successful adults who can help heal our nation's divisions rather than deepen them," said Florida Education Association president Andrew Spar in a press statement.[22]

In response to Florida's rejection of the AP curriculum for African American studies, NAACP director of education innovation and research Ivory Toldson said that Ron DeSantis' flippant dismissal was not only a "dereliction of his duty to ensure equitable education for all Floridians, but shows clear disdain for the lives and experiences that form part of our national history. Dismissing this important subject as lacking 'educational value' defies centuries of evidence to the contrary. African American history is American history, and failure to comprehend this very simple fact is un-American in and of itself."[23]

On their face, the reasons offered for passing bans on CRT made little to no sense. Although Republican-controlled legislatures proposed to limit the study of CRT, more than 96 percent of teachers said their schools did not require them to teach it, according to a survey by the nonpartisan membership organization the Association of American Educators.[24] To the claim that critical race theory fosters cynicism among Black people toward white politicians, the answer is that racism and white supremacy accomplished that. Instead, critical race theory reflects the lived reality of housing and employment discrimination, empirically confirmed by the country's inequitable distribution of privileges and burdens.

As states passed CRT legislation, the country also experienced a rise in book bans, targeting titles that were supposedly woke. According to PEN America, the campaign to limit access to books was propelled by "a vocal minority demanding censorship." In their findings, the group recorded 3,362 instances of book bans during the 2022–23 academic year, a notable increase from the 2,532 bans documented in the 2021–22 school year.[25]

Banning books during the age of Amazon makes little sense. The spotlight placed on the books can have the opposite effect and increase sales. In addition, as health policy researcher Ahmed Ali tweeted, "If Black children are old enough to experience racism, then other children are old enough to learn about critical race theory."[26] As long as there is racism, there will be Black people finding ways to understand and dismantle it.

Black people's ability to analyze systems and write books—on critical theory or any other subject—reflects rising power. In response, conservatives pushed prohibitions as a vehicle to mobilize constituents around throttling Black power. Education provided a foil to open a new front in the evergreen culture wars, engage their base, and lay another plank in the party's anti-Black platform.

As Florida Democratic senator Shevrin Jones said, "Gov. DeSantis' whitewashing of history and book bans are his latest assault on American history and our First Amendment rights. Horrifyingly, it is our vulnerable and underrepresented students who will suffer the most as a result."[27] Jones is only partially right: these anti-education efforts that are seeking to curb Black power also throttle educational growth among white people.

While we wring our hands over the lagging educational achievements of Black, Latino, and Native students, these campaigns remind us that there is an education crisis among white students in America, too. According to the latest NAEP results, white students demonstrate a limited understanding of history, scoring twenty-two points below the minimum level of achievement, or "cut score," on the NAEP US history exam. Keeping Americans from learning foundational lessons about history, social studies, and civics impedes their comprehension of the origins of systemic racism and the use of race to fragment American society and consolidate power.

The failure of white people to confront the cognitive dissonance that results from denying racism contributes to societal divisions. Receiving an incomplete or sanitized history of slavery, the Civil War, the Confederacy, and segregation not only hinders students' grasp of the American past but also robs them of critical thinking. There is also the fact that racist children tend to become racist adults. As Shevrin Jones noted, the willful ignorance of the powerful means a greater burden on the less powerful. Ignorance is not bliss when it comes to economic competitiveness and strengthening democracy. State and national economies are hindered when citizens are dumbed down.

Education wars are being waged on a larger political stage to rally communities around values for which they are willing to sacrifice basic facts. This same stage can serve Black communities to rally instead to advance schools and universities and shared goals of wealth, knowledge, and dignity.

* * *

ON SATURDAYS IN New Orleans, you can find children and adults in playgrounds and sports stadiums working with microscopes, cell counters, beakers, batteries, stethoscopes, and blood pressure monitors. On one particular weekend, the participants of STEM NOLA built model cities and levees to learn about coastal erosion and hurricane protection.

"In New Orleans, it doesn't make sense to teach certain scientific concepts through a volcano when you can use Lake Pontchartrain," Calvin Mackie said, referring to the lake that surged and flooded much of the city during Hurricane Katrina. "Education has to be portable, organic, and relevant."

Just as it's easier to learn French in France, it's more effective to teach civics, literature, and science in the context of communities. Opportunities for students to practice what they are hopefully learning in schools are invaluable. And New Orleans, which experienced the greatest engineering and social service disaster in the country's history when its levee system failed, could stand to produce a few engineers from the hood.

Mackie is harnessing the physical landscape and bolstering the educational environment when school is closed, at the same time remediating dangerous spaces that are vulnerable to inadequate or overpolicing and violence. The purpose of STEM NOLA is "to grow, engage, expose and inspire future innovators, creators, makers and entrepreneurs. Members of the community will learn about opportunities in the fields of Science, Technology, Engineering and Math." Crucially, his efforts are place-based, wealth-generating strategies for the Black community.

Mackie operates STEM NOLA out of Xavier University of Louisiana, a historically Black institution. Within a decade, STEM NOLA has "engaged 100,000 students starting in pre-kindergarten, 20,000 families and 2,150 schools across the United States and in five other countries, as well as countless STEM professionals," according to reporting from BizNOLA.[28] With great demand and to address the logistic challenges of holding events across the city, in 2022 Mackie started planning a forty-thousand-square-foot innovation hub in New Orleans East to provide resources and technology for students pursuing STEM careers.

Mackie has incorporated the economic development efforts of his superhero brother, film actor Anthony Mackie, who plays Falcon in the Marvel cinematic universe.[29] Anthony Mackie acquired twenty acres of land nearly across the street from his older brother's facility to establish East Studios LLC movie studio.[30] Between the two, the Mackie brothers are developing a comprehensive project to transform an abandoned area into a vibrant cultural district. By integrating education, entrepreneurship, and community development, the Mackies aim to spur positive change and promote opportunities for residents in New Orleans East.

Calvin Mackie also understands the need to combat the entrenched narratives, particularly that Black boys and men are inherently criminal, something that's easier when you have a superhero on your side. "We live in a country right now that makes sure every Black and Brown boy touches a football before the age of four," he said in an interview.[31] That's part of the narrative, and instead, he wants every child to touch a scientific instrument before they touch a football.

Mackie represents a new wave of school founders emerging across the country, people who are building broader educational opportunities because they understand that a school is supposed to engage with the whole child and its community. They see the idea that education can only be found in a brick-and-mortar school as myopic as the notion that we can jail our way to safety. Notwithstanding the contributions of traditional school leaders, these founders are reshaping the educational landscape, generating wealth, and shifting narratives in the process.

Montgomery, Alabama, is probably better known for racial injustice than for innovation in education. However, through his Equal Justice Initiative, lawyer and civil rights leader Bryan Stevenson is dramatically reshaping the educational environment. Montgomery's Legacy Sites, which include the Legacy Museum, the National Memorial for Peace and Justice, and the Freedom Monument Sculpture Park, collectively represent reformed spaces where visitors confront America's history of racial injustice. These locations, with their profound historical significance, offer important opportunities for people to engage with the past and initiate conversations centered on truth and reconciliation.

The Legacy Museum, set in a former cotton warehouse where enslaved people once toiled, guides visitors through a compelling account of slavery and its enduring impact through immersive exhibits and storytelling. The National Memorial for Peace and Justice sits magnificently atop a hill in Montgomery, commemorating the legacy of enslaved Black Americans subjected to lynching, racial segregation, and systemic prejudice, honoring over 4,400 lives lost to lynchings. The Freedom Monument Sculpture Park, an immersive seventeen-acre site along the river, once a location for trafficking enslaved Africans, displays art, artifacts, and interactive features that shed light on the lived experiences of those who endured enslavement.

Another figure reshaping narratives in Alabama is Michelle Browder, an artist and entrepreneur, who is working to bring recognition to enslaved women who played a key role in medical advancements. From 1845 to 1849, Dr. J. Marion Sims, an Alabama surgeon, conducted experiments on enslaved Black women, among them Anarcha, Lucy, and Betsey, to develop effective treatment for vesicovaginal fistula, which posed a significant threat to health after childbirth. The concept of consent did not exist for this vulnerable population, and the stories of these women had gone largely ignored.

The surgeries and research that led to Sims's medical discoveries took place at 33 South Perry Street in Montgomery, close to a statue honoring Sims at the state capitol.

Browder acquired the building with the intention of converting it to the Mothers of Gynecology Health and Wellness Clinic, a $5.5 million facility encompassing a museum, treatment center, and training resource for medical professionals such as gynecologists, doulas, and midwives.

Browder is also responsible for the Mothers of Gynecology monument, which shows representations of Anarcha, Lucy, and Betsey crafted from scrap metal, bike chains, and other discarded materials. This tribute symbolizes the value of women whose bodies were often seen as expendable, now transformed and worthy of commemoration. The statue of Anarcha reaches to fifteen feet. In addition, Browder created the More Up Travel Center, which is designed to accommodate thirty-two guests and offers educational opportunities for travelers and activists in Montgomery, along with the Creative Changemakers Museum, "an innovative experience of art and history."

All these facilities not only add to the educational environment; they create jobs, involve land and property ownership, and they shift narratives. We should hold all formal educational institutions to the same standard.

Although wealth is an important driver of educational outcomes and choices, education reform efforts generally sidestep the issue, essentially telling people to turn off the stove when the house is already on fire. To detach scholastic achievement from the political economy is academically and morally irresponsible. Isolating student learning from their larger context insidiously removes our responsibility for improving children's homes, neighborhoods, and families. In response, communities have devised innovative means to enhance education in majority Black neighborhoods through libraries, mobile schools, recreational activities, dance programs, and other services that can operate in violent hot spots.

One important measure that would improve academic results, particularly in lower income areas, is to facilitate more time on educational tasks beyond regular school hours. Within the realm of formal education, the concept of extended learning time has emerged as a crucial strategy, something advocated by the Learning Policy Institute to address disparities and bridge achievement gaps.[32] Without additional time and exposure to quality learning opportunities, offered in targeted programs before and after standard classes, there is no way to bring Black students up to speed in the confines of the traditional school day and year.

The state of Massachusetts developed its Expanded Learning Time initiative in 2005 to enable selected schools to reimagine their schedules by extending their learning hours. Participating schools were required to increase learning time by a minimum of three hundred hours annually, focusing on enhancing performance in core academic subjects, fostering enrichment opportunities, and bolstering instructional quality through greater planning and professional development for educators.

Based on an independent evaluation, notable outcomes include significant improvements in fifth-grade science scores, more teacher focus on English language arts and math instruction, and improvements in pedagogical practices due to the extra learning time.[33] Stakeholders reported positive responses, with teachers expressing support for the initiative despite challenges related to resource constraints.

The nonprofit advocacy group Education Trust recommends increasing learning time with a focus on high-quality curriculum, small class sizes, and certified teachers, but doing so during the regular school year. Education Trust believes that adding between forty-five and one hundred hours in the school year can create conducive learning environments that maximize the development of students' skills.[34]

High-dose tutoring has also proven to be a highly effective approach to uplifting achievement.[35] On average, these programs help a student jump from performing at an average level to exceeding the performance of almost two-thirds of their peers. Programs led by teachers or trained tutors tend to be more effective than those led by volunteers or parents. Tutoring works best for younger students, but it can also help those in high school. Reading tutoring is best for younger children, while math tutoring is more effective for those who are slightly older. Tutoring programs offered during the school day usually work better than sessions held after school. Programs with less impact used parents as tutors or were held after school, making it harder to guarantee that the extra help was consistently valuable.

* * *

As CALVIN MACKIE knows, children don't live in schools; they live with families in neighborhoods. To support what is learned in schools, students need educationally and economically enriched neighborhoods. We shouldn't look to schools as our only or even primary source of learning. Education philosopher John Dewey said it best: "Education is not preparation for life; education is life itself." We need to fill the classrooms of our daily lives with varied kinds of learning, supporting all kinds of teachers who help students acquire knowledge while unlearning the narratives they have been exposed to.

Ultimately, the goal of Black power movements is to create environments that maximize human potential. In the context of education, that means articulating explicit goals to enhance learning for an improved quality of life and positive self-perception, and formulating political objectives to address the control of resources, which are key to educational growth. These goals should be able of address fundamental questions: How does this reform improve academic outcomes? How will it enhance employment and contracting opportunities? How does it increase in-school and out-of-school options? How does it alter narratives? These are inherently political aims that are often overlooked or even shunned.

Black power movements should be strategic about increasing learning opportunities in specific geographic areas. The importance of playgrounds, museums, libraries, and laboratories should interrupt educationally barren stretches of land. Education policies influence where we live, how we vote, and how we collect and distribute taxes. The built environment—the man-made structures and facilities in which people work and live and study—has been shaped by segregation and exploitation. To keep our heads down in a school and just strive to educate children to the best of our ability is to work within the confines of structured inequality. Education for Black power sees the connections between schools and colleges to systems of inequality and seeks freedom from those systems.

In school board meetings across the country, people

routinely reject political discussions in the context of education, saying that schools should just be "all about the kids." Avoiding political conversations related to education means sidestepping key discussions on resource allocation and undermining the role adults play in determining resources for Black communities. It is societies, not schools, that have the power to enact reform, and they do so on a political stage, where fundamental concepts of citizenship, social justice, and economic freedom are deliberated, implemented, and clarified.

Those who argue that politics have no place in education are people who have the luxury to ignore the role that politics play. More than likely, the people who make that claim are playing politics. Debates around who gets what, when, and how are as important in education as discussions of curriculum and instruction. Black power movements make the connection between the means and ends of education.

EMPOWERMENT THROUGH UNITY

No contract? No peace!
No justice? No Jeeps!
No pay? No parts!
No deal? No wheels![1]

Picketers lined the streets outside auto factories across the country shouting car-themed protest chants. Members of the United Auto Workers (UAW) union took themselves off different stages of the production lines in different cities, strategically shutting down the "Big Three" major assembly plants at Ford, General Motors, and Stellantis (formerly Chrysler).[2] Catching managers by surprise, workers set up the pickets on an hour's notice. "No justice? No Jeeps!" made it plain that there would be no cars (or profits) without a new labor agreement.

The UAW members had left their posts to demand significant improvements in compensation and benefits. They sought a 46 percent wage increase over a four-year contract. UAW employees started at $18 an hour, with peak pay at

$32.[3] The union proposed a hike to raise the wage floor substantially and reintroduce a cost-of-living allowance tied to inflation, a benefit discontinued in 2007 due to the auto industry crisis at the time. They also advocated the restoration of benefits lost before the 2009 recession, when GM and Chrysler faced bankruptcy, including reinstating traditional pensions and retiree health care, and reducing the workweek to thirty-two hours from forty. Additionally, the union wanted to limit the use of temporary workers and expedite their progression to full pay and benefits.

UAW president Shawn Fain called the demands "the most audacious list of proposals" in decades, aimed at compensating for past concessions from the union that had led to the companies enjoying record profits.[4]

At the heart of most labor disputes is compensation. In recent years, workers have clamored for a larger slice of the substantial profits made by companies to better match the rising cost of living. Ford, General Motors, and Stellantis saw their profits soar by 92 percent from 2013 to 2022, amassing $250 billion, with projections for 2023 forecasting over $32 billion more.[5] Despite this financial boon, where CEO pay surged by 40 percent and nearly $66 billion was directed toward shareholder dividends and stock buybacks, worker compensation had not seen comparable growth. After the strike, the combination of wages and benefits for Detroit's Big Three stands at an average of $64 an hour. In contrast, nonunion plants of international automakers like Toyota report labor costs at around $55 an hour, while Tesla's costs range from $45 to $50 an hour. This stark disparity between union and nonunion pay has driven labor's push for more consistency across companies, besides aligning more closely with the auto industry's profits and the escalating cost of living.

* * *

THE STRUGGLE FOR equitable pay in the automotive industry highlights the broader issue of income disparity, which affects societal outcomes, notably in health and longevity. Among the thirteen components of the Black Progress Index, income has the second-most significant positive impact on life expectancy: with each increase in income level, Black people's expected lifespan extends by approximately eight months. Income is one of the most important sources of Black wealth as well as a foundational structural element of society; it is a function of the laws, policies, and practices that enhance the economy's productive capacity and augment its flexibility.

The Black Progress Index offers a revealing insight into the wide wage disparities that exist in the United States, indicating the level of prosperity and health in counties with the highest and lowest average earnings for Black Americans. In counties like Loudoun, Virginia, and Wright, Minnesota, where Black household median incomes soar above $120,000, the correlation between financial security and longevity is undeniable. These regions not only feature substantial median incomes but also have high Black Progress Index scores and impressive life expectancies—confirming the strong link between economic success and healthier lives. Loudoun County's median Black income of $126,502 is coupled with an 82.4-year life expectancy. The Black-majority place with the highest incomes is Charles County, Maryland, hovering just over the six-figure mark at $101,269. Residents of Black-majority cities and counties in Maryland enjoy higher incomes in general. In 2017, Black incomes outpaced the national average in 124 Black-majority cities and about half were in Maryland.[6]

The other end of the spectrum exposes a starkly different reality. Bibb County, Alabama, has a median Black income of $14,591 and a life expectancy of 72.3; Amite County, Mississippi, with $14,394 and a life expectancy of 73.9; and Butler County, Missouri, with $15,893 and a significantly reduced life expectancy of 66.3 years, paint a picture of economic hardship. In most instances, lower incomes correlate with lower life expectancies.

What we might call a basic income is one that provides economic security, enabling people to realize their maximum lifespan potential. But the stark discrepancy in life expectancies between the richest and poorest Americans shows that incomes among the lowest-paid workers do not reach that basic level. There is no reason why autoworkers, store clerks, teachers, and sanitation workers should not earn wages sufficient to live to their fullest potential, nor is there any reason why long lifespans should be reserved for the very wealthy, who also establish the pay rates of their employees.

Health outcomes track with racial wage gaps. In 2019, Black workers earned an average of $21.05 per hour, approximately 73.4 percent of the $28.66 earned by white workers, according to a study by the Economic Policy Institute. When broken down by gender, Black men earned $20.60, or 70.7 percent of the $29.13 average wage of white men, while Black women's earnings of $18.61 represented 83.3 percent of the $22.35 average wage for white women.

We have already noted that education doesn't eliminate racial wage gaps. Black workers with a high school diploma earned $16.37 per hour, roughly 81.7 percent of the $20.04 earned by white workers with similar educational attainment. Those with a college degree saw their earnings increase to $27.81, but this still amounted to only 77.5 percent of the $35.90 earned by white college graduates. The gap persisted among those with advanced degrees, with Black workers earning $37.33, or 82.4 percent of the $45.29 earned by their white counterparts. These statistics illustrate the pervasive wage disparities based on race across all levels.

Examining the wage distribution reveals a clear pattern: at the 10th percentile, Black workers earned $9.61, which amounts to 91 percent of the $10.56 that white workers earned. The wage in the middle or median among all Black workers was $16.12, representing 75.6 percent of the white median wage of $21.32. The disparity becomes particularly pronounced at the 95th percentile, where Black workers earned $47.94, just 65.3 percent of the $73.38 earned by white workers in the same wage bracket.

Black people of different socioeconomic classes should be united in closing wage disparities. Economic Policy Institute researchers point out that the gap is less significant at the lower end of the spectrum, thanks to minimum wage laws that help prevent the poorest-paid Black workers from earning even less. But the gap significantly diverges at the upper end of the spectrum, partly due to the underrepresentation of Black people in high-paying professions.

* * *

In the United States, most people earn income from salaried employment or self-employment, with a smaller portion deriving income from government benefits. Even fewer people acquire unearned income from sources like inheritances, capital gains, or qualified dividends. Hence addressing wages and engaging with employers are crucial steps for Black individuals to empower themselves, which won't occur without a fight.

Profit maximization is at odds with ensuring workers have the incomes that enable them to live longer lives, and corporate executives assume they have an obligation to increase corporate profits and shareholder value. This culture is evident in rising disparities between executive pay, shareholder returns, and worker pay. However, Lynn Stout, distinguished professor of corporate and business law at Cornell Law School, disagrees with this position, citing the US Supreme Court opinion in *Burwell v. Hobby Lobby Stores* in 2014: "Modern corporate law does not require for-profit corporations to pursue profit at the expense of everything else, and many do not."[7]

In the view of Afro-pessimism, shareholder value can only come at the expense of Black lives. Frank B. Wilderson III, professor of African American studies at the University of California, Irvine, and author of *Afro-Pessimism*,[8] posits a structural analysis of human experience in which the devaluation of Black people is essential to corporate and societal growth. The concept draws on the historic impact of slavery on society, making exploitation a permanent feature. In its extreme form Afro-pessimism holds that "the spectacle of Black death is essential to the mental health of the world."[9] Afro-pessimism offers a critical lens through which to understand ingrained depth of exploitation in the United States and how resistant people are to setting pay tables in ways that value Black people's labor.

This philosophical stance helps explain why the struggle for equitable wages is particularly arduous for Black workers. To be clear, the uphill battle for higher wages is not aimed at achieving parity with white workers but rather at ensuring an income that affirms the dignity and value of Black lives—a societal shift that would be as monumental as discovering a cure for cancer. And this struggle for fair compensation is not just as an economic issue but a moral imperative, one that could lead to increased longevity and improved quality of life for Black communities.

This push toward redefining the value of work and worker compensation has found tangible expression in recent labor movements. Despite the decline in overall union membership from 20.1 percent in 1983 to 10.0 percent in 2023, unionization is meeting the moment, according to analysis by the Economic Policy Institute.[10] In 2022, two hundred thousand more workers were represented by a union than in 2021. Union activity across various sectors has seen a marked increase, including the unionization of the first Starbucks in Buffalo, New York, in December 2021, the largest higher education strike by University of California workers, and substantial wage victories for Walt Disney World hourly workers and American Airlines pilots. Labor organizations are gaining momentum nationwide.

After negotiations lasting about six weeks, the autoworkers' strike culminated in tentative agreements with all three of the big companies by late October 2023. These negotiations led to significant victories, such as a

33 percent wage increase, inclusive of raises and cost-of-living adjustments, for top-scale assembly plant workers,[11] who achieved immediate 11 percent raises, resulting in an hourly pay rate of approximately $42 by April 2028, when the contracts end. This outcome was widely celebrated as a win for the workers, symbolizing a significant step toward rectifying long-standing wage disparities and setting a new standard for just compensation in the labor market.

Lynne Vincent, a labor expert at Syracuse University, shared with CBS MoneyWatch the special approach taken by the UAW, "In a twist on the phrase 'collective bargaining,' the UAW's strategy to negotiate with and strike at the three automakers simultaneously paid off with seemingly strong agreements at all three organizations." She explained the UAW's strategic advantage: "Once a deal was reached at Ford, the UAW could use that agreement as the pattern for the other two automakers, which gave the UAW leverage to apply pressure."

For Black Americans, this kind of proactive, coordinated movement is a necessity, along with a set of income targets aimed at enhancing life expectancy and empowering people to reach their full potential. Black Americans and descendants of the enslaved have good reason to expect employers to prioritize profit maximization over their well-being and lifespan. Given that their incomes often originate from employers who view exploitation as a cornerstone of their operational model, a movement focused on unionism and collective action is essential. This movement should advocate for explicit income improvements that not only bridge existing wage gaps but also align with broader goals for equality and societal progress.

* * *

IN THE SPRING of 2021, an unprecedented event unfolded at the Amazon warehouse in Bessemer, Alabama, where 5,805 employees were presented with a monumental choice: whether to be represented by the Retail, Wholesale and Department Store Union. This marked the first instance in seven years that workers at the e-commerce behemoth had the opportunity to vote on such a matter. The vote, one year into the global pandemic, emerged during a critical juncture not just for Amazon employees but for the workforce at large. However, many felt it wasn't the right time to unionize.

JC Thompson, a pastor and Amazon worker at the Bessemer warehouse, shared his views in a Vice News interview.[12] "Some people will take this and say I'm anti-union. I'm not anti-union," Thompson said. "I believe that there is a place for unions in certain situations, but I just don't feel at Amazon, at this moment, there is a need because everything that a union would possibly fight for, we already have. At Amazon, we walk in the door, the ground level is $15 an hour. I have a 401k. I have medical, dental, vision [benefits]. I get a raise every six months. So, I'm asking myself what else can the union actually offer?"

The pandemic had endowed employees across many sectors with unprecedented bargaining power. During the Great Resignation that followed the pandemic, workers, particularly in blue-collar roles, opted to leave their positions in search of enhanced compensation and better conditions, thereby exerting pressure on employers to respond to escalating labor demands. For Amazon, the world's second-largest company after Walmart, the stakes were exceptionally high. The move toward unionization in Bessemer threatened to set a precedent that could inspire similar initiatives across its network, challenging the company's profit-driven operations model at its core.

In the financial year of 2020, Amazon enjoyed a dramatic surge in profitability due to the population's reliance on delivered goods, with returns jumping to an additional $9.7 billion, marking a staggering 84 percent increase from the prior year.[13] This financial boon was mirrored in the company's stock value, which escalated by 82 percent, and bolstered the wealth of its founder, Jeff Bezos, by $67.9 billion. Down the assembly line, Amazon's frontline employees received an average pay increase of roughly $0.99 per hour, equivalent to about a 7 percent raise. When compared to the pandemic-induced pay enhancements at competitor Costco, Amazon's pay bump—less than half of Costco's increase—appeared modest, underscoring how the e-commerce giant fails to reallocate profits toward workforce compensation.

The push for unionization at Amazon also came in the aftermath of the killing of George Floyd in Minneapolis, when corporations collectively pledged billions toward racial justice.[14] Philanthropic giving at the time was partly an expression of sympathy, partly a recognition of corporate America's role in exacting racial justice, and partly a response to the largest protest movement in the country's history.[15]

A significant portion of Amazon's workforce, 27 percent, is made up of Black employees, a figure that notably exceeds the representation of Black workers in the general

US workforce at 13 percent. Their presence is particularly pronounced at the Bessemer warehouse, where they are estimated to make up 85 percent of the employees, situating the unionization efforts within a charged sociopolitical milieu. The backdrop of the South, a region where right-to-work laws predominate, prohibiting certain forms of collective bargaining, added another layer of complexity to the union initiative, reflecting the intertwined issues of labor rights, racial justice, and economic equity.

The geographical distribution of union membership tells a story of unexploited opportunities for Black workers in states with historically low rates of unionization. While states like New York and Hawaii show significantly higher membership rates, offering a blueprint for the benefits of strong union presence, southern states with large Black populations—and correspondingly low union rates—highlight regions where the potential gains from increased unionization are greatest.[16] This uneven distribution suggests a strategic direction for organizing efforts: focusing on areas where Black workers stand to gain the most from collective bargaining.

Unions significantly boost wages. According to the US Bureau of Labor Statistics, union workers enjoy median weekly earnings that are markedly higher than those of their nonunion peers. The median weekly earnings of nonunion workers were 86 percent of those for workers with union membership ($1,090 versus $1,263).[17] This disparity is even more pronounced among Black unionized workers, who see a larger wage premium compared to their white counterparts, demonstrating how collective bargaining can directly counter wage inequalities that disproportionally affect Black employees.

Union membership offers a path to better benefits and job stability. Unions negotiate not only for higher wages but also comprehensive benefits packages that include health insurance, retirement plans, and paid leave—amenities less commonly found in nonunion workplaces, particularly those employing large numbers of Black workers. Additionally, the job security afforded by union representation is crucial in sectors known for high turnover rates and precarious employment conditions, safeguarding workers against unjust termination and ensuring greater stability for Black families.

Since its inception in 1994, Amazon has consistently deterred efforts to unionize its workforce, deploying strategies that range from closely monitoring employee activism on platforms like listservs and social media groups to developing a robust anti-union stance.[18] The National Labor Relations Board has flagged Amazon for engaging in illegal anti-union practices, including the retaliatory firing of workers advocating for unionization.[19]

Union organizers charged Amazon with hiring vulnerable employees like formerly incarcerated individuals to help spread anti-union messaging. In the *American Prospect*, RWDSU organizer Michael Foster, affectionately known as "Big Mike," expressed empathy toward these individuals, whom he dubbed "a walking billboard" for Amazon's anti-union activity.[20] Foster said, "You got these guys just getting out of being incarcerated, so it's hard for them to find employment. Amazon is preying upon their downfall." Economic and social vulnerability often presents Black people with little option but to accept the status quo. Any job becomes a good job.

During the pandemic, the long-standing reality that Black people are more likely to work in low-wage, dangerous jobs came into sharp focus, along with the terms *essential* and *frontline workers*. Although the terms became staples in discussions about workplace safety and public health, the designations are informal; there is no legal definition for who qualifies as such.[21] However, an essential industry is almost universally understood to encompass businesses and establishments deemed crucial enough to remain operational during a public health emergency. The services or goods provided by these industries are vital for the continued functioning of society and must be sustained even when other sectors are paused or significantly reduced to mitigate health risks. Essential or frontline employees are those who work in these industries, people who continue to report in person to their jobs despite uncertain and potentially significant risks to their physical health.[22]

Throughout the COVID-19 pandemic, analysts and media commentators found Black workers overrepresented in the ranks of frontline, essential workers—among them bus drivers, security staff, and hospital support personnel. These roles were precarious, threatening both the workers' health and that of their families, while failing to provide a wage that meets basic needs. Despite comprising only 13 percent of the country's workforce, Black employees accounted for nearly 19 percent of those in essential roles paying less than $16.54 an hour—the minimum amount deemed necessary to support a family of four.[23]

Black people don't just happen to find themselves in jobs that offer lower pay. They are subject to occupational segregation, a process where employers and workers allocate jobs based on societal norms. Black labor is devalued in the same way that homes in Black neighborhoods are undervalued: paradoxically termed "essential," they are worth much more than their pay suggests. In his 1968 speech "All Labor Has Dignity," given during a sanitation strike in Memphis, Tennessee, Martin Luther King Jr. highlighted this point: "So often we overlook the work and significance of those not in professional or so-called big jobs. But let me tell you . . . work that serves humanity and contributes to the building of humanity holds dignity and worth."[24] The devaluation of certain workers (Black people and women) leads to reduced compensation.

There are different ideas of what constitutes an adequate income. One is the *minimum wage*, the lowest amount an employer can legally pay, which is intended as a safeguard to prevent earnings from falling below a level deemed too low.[25] However, data from the Living Wage Institute shows that the minimum wage, which is mostly designated by state legislators, often fails to cover the actual costs of living for families, leading to situations where working adults must rely on public assistance or take on multiple jobs to afford basic necessities like food, clothing, housing, and health care.[26]

In contrast, a *living wage* is a calculated income level that allows individuals and families to cover their basic needs without additional financial assistance, aiming to provide financial independence and security. It takes the actual costs of living into account, including essentials such as housing, food, childcare, health care, and transportation. A living wage not only ensures the ability to meet daily expenses, it also offers opportunities for savings, investments, and purchasing assets like homes, contributing to wealth building and long-term economic stability.

The Living Wage Institute calculated living wage for a typical family of four (two working adults, two children) in December 2022 was estimated to be $25.02 per hour, or an annual income of $104,077.70 before taxes. This reflects an increase from 2021, when the living wage was assessed at $24.16 per hour, or $100,498.60 annually. This starkly contrasts with the federal minimum wage of $7.25 per hour, which is insufficient for most American families to live on without additional jobs or assistance. Specifically, to earn a living wage, a family of four would need to work significantly more than two full-time minimum-wage jobs—a combined effort equating to a ninety-six-hour workweek per working adult. For single-parent families, the effort required nearly doubles, with a single mother of two needing to work the equivalent of almost six full-time minimum-wage jobs, or 252 hours per week, to reach a living wage.

The devaluation of Black labor not only affects individuals but also contributes to broader economic inequality, as highlighted by the stark differences between minimum-wage standards and a living wage. For Black workers, a living wage is a worthy organizing goal, reflecting the pursuit of financial independence, economic stability, and the opportunity for families to meet their daily needs but also build wealth and secure a better future.

Amazon workers in Bessemer eventually voted decisively (not once but twice) against forming a union. In

April 2021, 1,798 workers rejected the unionization effort. Only 738 workers, representing less than 30 percent of the total votes cast, voted in favor.[27] However, the National Labor Relations Board found that Amazon had improperly interfered in the election, forcing a second.[28] This vote proved closer but still tilted against forming a union: 993 voted against joining RWDSU labor union with 875 in favor.[29]

Regardless of the outcome of any one union election, the recalibration of the value of Black workers is a core part of redressing historical exploitation. The ways in which skills and occupations are valued, especially in the South, along with anti-labor laws and suppressed income levels, are deeply intertwined with the long oppression of Black labor. Racism, manifested through the exploitation of no- or low-wage Black work, has had a profound influence on the development of norms and salary standards across industries. The economic pressures on laborers to accept less than what they are owed is often too great to expect someone to vote for the good of the greater community.

Individuals tend to compare their wages to those of workers in other places and companies, which is a fraught comparison because those workers often have good reason to feel compelled to accept less than a living wage due to limited choices and opportunities. Being offered double the rate of pay as well as benefits and retirement to work at Amazon might seem like a good deal and lack of exploitation.

"What really gets me is how the news talks like we get $60 or $70 an hour," said Kim Forschim, an auto assembly worker, to the pro-union media outfit Labor Notes.[30] Forschim, who assembles front fascia on Chevy Colorado trucks at GM's Wentzville Assembly Center near St. Louis, Missouri, was registering her frustration with the way workers were being covered. "None of us make that! We get $32 an hour if we're lucky. New temps get $16 an hour and no raises, no vacation, no sick days. It's hard to live like that."

As long as Black workers collectively don't receive a living wage, they will lack the power to get the pay and benefits to live their life potential. At some point, Black workers must make demands that are commensurate with their lives and value.

* * *

As KING STATED in his speech "All Labor Has Dignity," "Let it be known everywhere that along with wages and all of the other securities that you are struggling for, you are also struggling for the right to organize and be recognized."

Society and employers won't come to respect Black workers on their own. If corporations fail to recognize their value, then Black people must join and establish unions and other organizations to leverage the power of the collective. Respect, dignity, and better wages will only come from a demand. While gaining higher incomes doesn't necessarily require mass union membership, living wages won't come without collective organizing and mobilizing by workers across different sectors and socioeconomic classes.

Given health and wealth disparities, wages need to be measured by whether they secure overall quality of life, both for individuals and their communities. The appropriate income is relative to a living wage that allows individuals and communities to fulfill their potential, rather than merely earning more than a worker at another company or region. As King asserted, "One day our society will come to respect the sanitation worker if it is to survive, for the person who picks up our garbage, in the final analysis, is as significant as the physician because, if he doesn't do his job, diseases become rampant." From the start, Black power movements fought to ensure fair wages, not only for current workers but also for the quality of life of future generations entering the workforce.

REPARATIONS
GO TO DC

In July 2023, Houston city officials declared their intention to begin the process of relocating residents from neighborhoods in the vicinity of the Union Pacific railyard, a notorious hot spot for cancer-causing pollutants.[1] For years, people who lived in the Kashmere Gardens and Fifth Ward neighborhoods in northeast Houston had been advocating for action to address contamination; state health authorities confirmed their concerns in a 2021 report identifying a heightened occurrence of lymphoblastic leukemia in children within a two-mile radius of the site.[2]

According to Houston Health Department director Stephen Williams, an alarming 79 percent of soil samples from the area surpassed the cancer risk thresholds set by the US Environmental Protection Agency, with the most contaminated sample exceeding the limit by over 1,900 times. Furthermore, EPA investigations identified four distinct cancer clusters and revealed childhood leukemia rates 350 percent above the national average.

"The creosote was so bad, you couldn't even open up

your window late at night when they turned those plants on," Sharon Elliott told ABC13 KTRK.[3] Elliott and her family had lived in the area for forty years. "It was really bad around here."

With a budget set between $24 million and $26 million, the city's relocation initiative marked a significant victory for members of the predominantly Black and Latino community, who had long been sounding the alarm about the unusually high illness and mortality rates in their living area.

"Time is the enemy for people living in the highly exposed and dangerous zone," Mayor Sylvester Turner said during a press conference, announcing the plan.[4]

Following the findings, in 2023, the agency and Union Pacific reached a legal settlement compelling the corporation to launch a thorough investigation into the contamination at the railyard site. However, the company did not announce that it would join the city in paying for the relocations.

Formulating a plan to get residents out of harm's way is undeniably a responsibility of local government, but corporate action clearly contributed to the harm, and there is a case to be made that Union Pacific bore partial responsibility for relocating the residents. The city's plan also amounted to a tacit recognition that the government, through its implementation of specific permitting and zoning regulations, tolerated its citizens living in situations so dangerous that they necessitate remedial action and accountability.

By definition, providing money for residents' relocation is a form of local reparations—a system of redress for egregious injustice. The city of Houston did not call its program reparations, but the move came at a time when residents of cities and states across the nation are calling for local jurisdictions to be accountable for past injustice, and in some cases they are winning what they consider to be reparations.

Almost four hundred years after Massachusetts recognized slavery as a legal institution, Boston is seeking to repair the harm caused by its participation in the transatlantic slave trade through its Task Force on Reparations, which is dedicated to researching the lasting impact of slavery.[5] California's Task Force to Study and Develop Reparations Proposals for African Americans has presented more than one hundred recommendations for a reparations program on the state level, leaving it up to state legislators to implement them. In 2019, Evanston, Illinois, made history by enacting the first reparations legislation in the country, aimed specifically at combating the effects of segregationist housing policies by offering $25,000 grants for home improvements to Black residents who had lived in the city since before 1969.

There is a critical view among some experts, including Duke University economist William A. Darity Jr. and folklorist and museum consultant A. Kirsten Mullen, coauthors of *From Here to Equality: Reparations for Black Americans in the Twenty-First Century*, that these local initiatives serve as a distraction from a congressional act, which they consider the path needed to reach genuine reparations.[6]

To date, the United States has provided no form of reparations to the descendants of enslaved Black Americans for their ancestors' labor and suffering. Local efforts fall far short of compensation that would match the scale of harm caused by slavery, Darity and Mullen argue, contending that true redress requires bridging the national wealth gap between white and Black Americans. As one of the two most egregious acts of injustice in the United States—the other being the destruction of Native Americans—slavery warrants a program for reparations for descendants of the enslaved. However, the federal government has also not restored the equity lost from other egregious acts of discrimination, including in housing, transportation, and education, and it shares much of the culpability with states, municipalities, companies, and educational institutions. All these jurisdictions contributed to the racial wealth gap, which significantly impedes Black Americans' ability to self-determine. And injury caused by racial discrimination deserves redress if it closes a wealth gap or not. Numerous attempts have been made by members of Congress to introduce reparations legislation, with Democratic Representative Cori Bush of Missouri proposing a reparations package in 2023 of $14 trillion. The bill was intended to complement House Resolution 40, the Commission to Study and Develop Reparation Proposals for African Americans Act.[7] Since its introduction in 1989, H.R. 40 (named for forty acres and a mule) has been a recurring proposition in every legislative session. H.R. 40 finally advanced through the House Judiciary Committee in 2021, but was not brought to the floor for a vote in either the House or Senate.

While efforts to achieve reparations for slavery have moved very slowly, the actions by individual states and local governments have created momentum that might propel a national movement. If reparations won't come from Washington, they will go to Washington. They are building power from the ground up.

By demanding that cities, states, churches, companies, and universities hold themselves accountable for discrimination, activists are compelling these entities to acknowledge their liability for past harms. Local leaders are defining what reparations should look like while delivering restorative justice, including compensation, for Black Americans. These efforts to define and determine the rules of engagement around reparations are the ultimate measure of Black power. The two core questions at the heart of any reparations policy are who should qualify and how much should they receive. But the debate on these two issues, as it pertains to slavery, has generally brought the discussion to a grinding halt. I argue that the local reparations initiatives make those questions easier to answer than a national plan of redress for slavery. Less an issue of calculating amounts, local reparations movements have been able to focus on redressing the consequences of discrimination in immediate living conditions, which might be rooted in the past but determine people's lives today. In the case of Kashmere Gardens, it was clear that Fifth Ward residents had to be moved from the toxins that Houston allowed the railroad company to produce. Environmental justice addresses current living conditions while redressing past racial injustice and environmental degradation, making it a strong and effective vehicle for reparations.

* * *

THE UNITED NATIONS serves as a legal instrument for international law, to which UN member states, including the United States, are obliged to adhere.[8] The UN charter outlines the key principles according to which nation-states should conduct themselves, principles ranging from the sovereign equality of states to a ban on using force in international affairs other than in self-defense. Accordingly, the UN provides fundamental principles that not only ground civic laws but also offer guidance for actions when basic human rights and protections are violated under those laws.

To that end, the UN makes clear that nation-states should provide reparations for breaches of human rights and effective mechanisms for the enforcement of judgments. Under UN guidelines for reparations, "victims of gross violations of international human rights law . . . should, as appropriate and proportional to the gravity of the violation and the circumstances of each case, be provided with full and effective reparation, . . . which include the following forms: restitution, compensation, rehabilitation, satisfaction and guarantees of non-repetition."[9] Individuals subjected to slavery, Jim Crow laws—including segregation and housing discrimination—and anti-Black criminal justice policies undoubtedly qualify as deserving of reparations, as these violations of human rights have stripped them of their fundamental freedoms and human dignity.

Restitution aims to, wherever feasible, return the victim to the state prior to the severe breach of international human rights.[10] *Compensation* should be offered for economically measurable losses, including employment, education, earnings, medical services, and moral damage. These two principles dominate the discussion on reparations, but there are other important aspects. *Rehabilitation* should include medical and psychological care, as well as legal and social services. *Satisfaction*, the recognition of fulfillment of reparations by the victims, includes a public apology, acknowledgment of the facts, and acceptance of responsibility. *Guarantees of non-repetition* should include legal assurances that the acts will not reoccur. In total, these components comprise reparations.

While significant attention is paid to discussion of the issues of restitution and compensation for slavery, not enough is given to the lack of guarantees for non-repetition evidenced by the human rights violations that Black people continue to live (and die) with.

The EPA defines a brownfield as a property whose "expansion, redevelopment, or reuse . . . may be complicated by the presence or potential presence of a hazardous substance, pollutant, or contaminant."[11] It estimates that there are more than 450,000 brownfields in the United States and notes that revitalizing these sites by cleaning and investing in them boosts local tax revenues, supports job creation, leverages existing infrastructure, reduces development pressure on open areas, and enhances as well as safeguards the environment. However, many people still live near or on these sites and are exposed to environs that are deleterious to health. Residents' proximity to brownfields is a human rights violation tied to racial discrimination.

"A safe, clean, healthy and sustainable environment is integral to the full enjoyment of a wide range of human rights, including the rights to life, health, food, water and sanitation," according to the UN.[12] "Without a healthy environment, we are unable to fulfil our aspirations."

This is certainly true of "Cancer Alley," an eighty-five-mile stretch along the Mississippi River in Louisiana, where Black residents have long faced higher rates of death and morbidity due to pollution and toxicity.

The EPA estimates that an astonishing fifty-eight million people live within one mile of a brownfield site (roughly 18 percent of the US population), including approximately 30 percent of all Black Americans, the largest of all groups. The high representation of Black people at such sites isn't a coincidence. The exploitation of African Americans that began with enslavement was deeply connected to environmental degradation, having been key to the process of turning the United States into the world's leading contributor to emissions and creating an unequal distribution of pollution. As the most lucrative industry of its era, slavery and its by-products generated immense wealth for the US economy, fostering rapid industrial expansion and extraction of resources.[13] At the same time, the colonization and seizure of more than 99 percent of Native lands further laid the groundwork for wealth accumulation among the white population.

This pattern continued as industrialization took the place of plantations, with heavy industry flourishing on land and infrastructure previously cultivated by the enslaved, subjecting many of the same communities and families to increased exposure to pollutants. Infrastructure and housing policies, such as redlining and the creation of white suburbs, exacerbated the process by segregating people of color in impoverished areas, trapping families in harmful conditions, partitioning Black neighborhoods with pollutant-emitting highways, restricting their access to green spaces, and denying them access to the same financial and social benefits as white Americans. Heavy industry and industrial polluters were frequently situated in Black majority and other minority areas and designated as "sacrifice zones." They bore the sacrifice for clean communities elsewhere.[14]

As a result, Black Americans in various regions of the country are far more likely to reside in close proximity to carcinogenic substances.

A recent inquiry by the EPA into Cancer Alley had the potential to be transformative, marking one of the few instances where the agency sought to apply the federal Civil Rights Act to address the inaction of state government, in this case Louisiana. Initial results connected state-level failures to remediate the environment to instances of toxic exposure. However, in June 2023, following a legal challenge by the state attorney general, Jeff Landry (who went on to become governor), the EPA terminated the case out of fear that the Supreme Court might respond by rolling back a significant tool in the arsenal to combat discrimination. The premature closure of the case halted a promising chance to enhance pollutant regulation and initiate discussions on compensation. In Texas, however, the city of Houston has sought to get residents out of harm's way, addressing (albeit not fully) key components of reparations. City officials have identified who is eligible and are providing compensation, answering the question of how much. In the area of concern with the creosote plume, there are approximately 110 land parcels, including sixty-one residential units housing forty-one residents. The rest of the parcels are occupied by small businesses and nonprofits. The city provided buyout options to those who own their homes outright or have mortgages, according to reporting by Houston Public Media.[15] The city introduced a forgivable loan program for homeowners: if the city purchases a property for $100,000 and constructs a new home for $150,000 with no additional cost involved, it results in a $50,000 debt for the homeowner. This debt will be pardoned, provided the owner resides in the new property for a minimum of three years. The homeowner can also choose to collaborate with one of the nonprofits involved to select a plot in a different area in the city and engage a builder in a process called a "dual closing." For renters, the city has offered $10,000 to move from the area. However, this compensation for moving doesn't address health care, employment losses, and other damages. Not only do these actions address compensatory issues, they also discourage repetition of the injury by setting a precedent. This is crucial: a company that pollutes during its operation and subsequently departs, leaving behind contaminated land, commits a recurring transgression. The very existence of brownfields underscores the absence of assurances for non-repetition.

Other cities across the country have ignored toxic exposure and the data that accompanies it. According to a 2020 EPA analysis of the population surrounding 27,030 brownfield sites, around twenty-seven million individuals, constituting roughly 8 percent of the US population, reside within half a mile of one. This includes approximately 9 percent of all children under the age of five, 8 percent of all children under eighteen, 15 percent of the Black population, 10 percent of Hispanics, 11 percent of minorities overall, 14 percent of households below the poverty line, 12 percent of individuals with less than a high school education, and 13 percent of linguistically isolated people. Included among the 18 percent of US residents who live within one mile of brownfield sites, in addition to the 30 percent of Black Americans, are 22 percent of Hispanics, 24 percent of all minorities, and 27 percent of households living below the poverty line.

To repeat Darity and Mullen's argument, "True reparations only can come from a full-scale program of acknowledgment, redress and closure for a grievous injustice."[16] While they claim that local efforts take momentum away from more sweeping initiatives at the federal level, looking at the scale of violation, even just in terms of brownfield sites, it is hard to see a scenario that provides a comprehensive plan of acknowledgment and accountability that leaves out past and present local officials.

The EPA's involvement in brownfield sites signal that there should be a federal response, but industry should not be let off the hook. In Houston, Union Pacific was the actual polluter, yet the company was not slated to help pay for the relocations.

Pamela Mathews and her family lived in Houston's Northeast neighborhood. During a press conference, Mathews said that she been part of the community since she was five. She lost her mother to cancer in 2022 and her brother was terminally ill. "Why should Union Pacific take all that money and harm all these people and not be held accountable?" asked Mathews.[17]

Houston's mayor, Sylvester Turner, echoed Mathews's point, calling on Union Pacific to join and financially support the initiative, believing that the company was morally obligated to act. "How many more people must be diagnosed with cancer?" he asked. "How many more people, and specifically how many more children, must die?" Through a spokesperson, Union Pacific stated that the company would wait to remediate the land until all the testing was completed. "Union Pacific will pay for what it is responsible for," said Toni Harrison. "Without a thorough comprehensive health risk assessment, we do not know which next steps are necessary."[18]

Many companies never rehabilitate polluted land, leaving it vacant and contaminated, and most do not relocate and compensate their victims. The city of Houston has owned some responsibility, but reparations for government and industry negligence ought to encompass more than rehousing and relocation costs. Families that relocate independently after seeing loved ones develop cancers and die should have the right to seek reimbursement as well as money for health-care costs. Relocation assistance falls short in tackling the enduring toxic effects on health as well as the long-lasting, multigenerational impact of restricting families to areas riddled with cancer-causing agents.

* * *

IN MICHIGAN, THE state's Department of Environment, Great Lakes, and Energy has played a key role in redeveloping Detroit by financing assessments and cleanups of brownfield sites. Various state and local administrations and community groups have utilized EPA brownfields grants, a federal program that provides direct funding for a variety of brownfield-related activities. Michigan environmental justice organizations have used this funding to rejuvenate contaminated properties and breathe new life into neighborhoods. As of February 2024, the EPA's Region 5 Brownfields Program (which includes Illinois, Indiana, Michigan, Minnesota, Ohio, and Wisconsin) had evaluated 3,270 properties, remediated eighty-eight sites, mobilized over $2.61 billion, and generated 21,602 job opportunities over the last nineteen years.[19]

The essence and spirit of Detroit and southeast Michigan are deeply connected to its manufacturing sector, forged through the work of its residents. By the mid-twentieth century, the automobile industry either directly or indirectly employed one out of six American workers, with Detroit at the heart of this sector.[20] The Big Three automotive companies had their headquarters in the Detroit metropolitan area. The auto industry's demand for steel, glass, copper, and later plastic led to the growth of numerous related industries within the city and its surroundings. At the conclusion of World War I, over eight thousand Black individuals were employed in Detroit's automobile sector, including 1,675 at Ford, according to research by the Henry Ford, a museum and education center.[21] A significant portion of Ford's Black workforce undertook roles such as janitors and cleaners, and were charged with tasks within the hazardous and grimy environments of the large blast furnaces and foundries. Black people were restricted to the least remunerative and most dangerous positions and had fewer options to leave their work conditions when compared to their white peers. By 1930, 14 percent of all autoworkers were Black and 80 percent of employed Black men worked in the plants.[22] The plants were often segregated, with the presence of Ku Klux Klan members within Detroit's factory workforce.

Regardless of race, foundry laborers were more likely to quit their jobs compared to workers in other positions at Ford, signifying that those roles were less desirable. When accounting for foundry positions, one 2003 study found that Black employees exhibited lower turnover rates than others, suggesting that they had fewer and less attractive opportunities.[23] The study also found that the wage and turnover rate data suggest systemic discrimination in the job market, leading Ford to exploit this disparity. Taking advantage of a market that discriminated against Black people, the company hired and paid relatively competitive wages, leveraging Black people's lack of options in the workplace to propel the company.

The rise in Black workers in Detroit aligned with a housing shortage in the city, which led to the emergence of discriminatory practices against Black families. This World War I period saw the establishment of clearly demarcated segregated residential zones and social amenities in the city.[24] The housing deficit was particularly challenging for Black laborers: a 1919 survey revealed a shortage of 33,000 living spaces and around 165,000 people dwelling in inadequate conditions. Black workers faced severe overcrowding and substandard living conditions, and in certain instances they struggled to secure suitable housing altogether.

As Detroit became one of the largest polluters in the world, it also became one of the most segregated communities with the rise of redlining in the 1930s. A 2022 study published in the *Journal of Exposure Science & Environmental Epidemiology* found that historically redlined areas in Detroit displayed notably elevated environmental risks compared to nonredlined regions, characterized by 12 percent higher levels of diesel particulate matter, 32 percent increased traffic activity, and 66 percent heightened exposure to harmful road noise.[25]

The 2022 *State of the Air* report by the American Lung Association indicates that Detroit's air quality has deteriorated, particularly in terms of particle pollution and ozone, with its ozone pollution rankings falling to make it the twenty-fourth most polluted area in the nation for 2018–2020.[26] The report serves as an annual assessment of air quality across the country, grading exposure to ground-level ozone and particle pollution over a three-year period. Air pollution has been linked to premature death, cardiovascular damage, and lung cancer, especially among vulnerable groups such as children, the elderly, and those with chronic diseases. This data comports with the Black Progress Index finding that air pollution, as measured by average daily density of fine particulate matter, is one of the largest drags on life expectancy for Black people.

Deindustrialization, decarbonization, depopulation, including white flight, and advancements in clean technology have reduced the amount of pollution in the region. However, over the decades, ozone pollution has been exacerbated by climate change.[27] The residual legacy of employment and environmental discrimination is literally still present in the brownfield sites in the region.

* * *

IN THE HEART of Detroit, the HOPE Village Revitalization project embarked on a mission to transform once-contaminated brownfields into thriving centers of community life. The vision was grand and the resources limited, but the determination was unwavering.

For centuries, Oakman Boulevard has borne witness to the rise and fall of industries, leaving behind a legacy of environmental ruin. HOPE Village saw potential where others saw only blight. Armed with grants and the innovative use of financing mechanisms, the organization set out to breathe new life into forgotten spaces.

The project's financial foundation was set upon a strategic blend of grants, loans, and tax increment financing, carefully selected to mitigate risks and entice private investments. The EPA Brownfields Cleanup Grant provided foundational federal support to bolster the remediation process. Additionally, the city of Detroit offered a Brownfields Revolving Loan, which can be used to bridge what a developer has in hand and what is needed to complete a project.

The size and scale of the environmental repairs demand government revenue. Pulls on city government's tax revenue are varied. So when it comes to new projects, cities must get creative. Tax increment financing allows cities to deploy tax revenue from a specified development project to finance additional development projects that are short on cash. Under Michigan's Act 381, tax increment

financing became a crucial tool in incentivizing redevelopment. The mechanism captured new tax revenues generated from the revitalization of brownfields, recycling
them to cover eligible costs, effectively sparking private
interest in the area.

In addition to federal and municipal support, HOPE
Village also benefited from state backing through the Cool
Cities initiative, which provides funding and an array of
"toolbox" resources from Michigan state agencies to assist
cities and neighborhoods in implementing the projects
detailed in their applications. In addition, HOPE Village
received support from nonprofit community development
organizations, including Detroit LISC and the Detroit
Brownfield Development Association, rounding out a
whole-of-community support for the redevelopment of
brownfields. With this braided funding, HOPE Village
revitalized several sites along Oakman Boulevard, including the Federal Engineering Building at 850 Oakman Boulevard, once contaminated with various pollutants, and a
former filling station, to create a productive green space,
Cool Cities Park, as a neighborhood meeting place and
walking path. The former Michigan Bell and Western Elec-
tric Warehouse was reconceived as supportive housing for
155 homeless individuals, a beacon of promise in a community yearning for stability.

Much of this financing resulted from the bundling of
dollars, some of which were intentionally aimed at racial
justice, some of them not. However bundled, HOPE Village Revitalization showed what a reparative fund for reha-
bilitating brownfields can look like. Its efforts were not just

focused on getting residents out of harm's way; it restored the people, the land, and community. By demonstrating what was possible, it also revealed what is owed.

What is owed is accessible, public green space. Trees, green roofs, and plant life mitigate the impact of urban heat islands by shading structures, reflecting sunlight, and introducing moisture into the air.[28] Urban green spaces improve neighborhood conditions by counterbalancing greenhouse gas emissions and channeling stormwater, allowing rainwater to replenish instead of flood.[29] Green space also allows residents to rejuvenate psychologically when areas that once caused cancer become healing spaces. Brownfields rob people of the possibility of exercise, relaxation, and socializing; they extract years of life, precious experiences, and beauty. Vacant toxic lots should be filled with nature, providing organic solace to heal generational traumas and microaggressions. Stress responses should be met with the sounds of birds instead of sirens.

What is owed is a home-building program that constructs affordable dwellings on rehabilitated brownfields, creating stable residences and job opportunities.[30] Hundreds of thousands of new homes would inject billions into the economy, also creating thousands of jobs. Communities that have been exposed to toxins deserve the security of safe, affordable homes in a place that allows for economic and social growth. These moribund brownfields present opportunities for innovative homeownership, offering collective options. A reparative culture would convert renters to owners who can grow equity to pass on to future generations. An increased housing supply would also help alleviate the escalating costs of homeownership, making it more accessible for a broader demographic. By leveraging brownfields for housing development, we would not only transform underutilized spaces but also construct the way for a more sustainable, inclusive, and prosperous future for our states and communities.

What is owed are lower energy bills. One insidious expression of racism is the vulnerability that lower wealth creates, including a lack of or failing HVAC systems in an overheating world. Incorporating renewable energy sources such as solar panels can lower utility bills and reduce reliance on traditional energy sources. Additionally, people living in areas heated by discrimination deserve insulation in their walls, floors, and attics to retain heat in the winter and cool the air during the summer. Older homes need upgrades to windows and doors to seal cracks and leaks. People deserve programs and initiatives that replace and repair failing heating and cooling systems. People are owed the ability to exercise better control over their heating and cooling systems through the installation of programmable thermostats. By optimizing energy usage based on daily schedules, these devices facilitate increased efficiency and reduced energy consumption for homeowners.

What is owed is access to good-paying jobs, recognizing that discrimination shows up in fewer opportunities to develop the skills needed to transition to lower-carbon economies, including green practices.[31] By prioritizing investments in green skill development among those subjected to environmental injustice, there would be an opportunity to equip them with valuable tools for success in an increasingly competitive job market. Government entities and former polluters must make targeted investments so that those disadvantaged by discrimination, particularly people with limited qualifications, are not left behind in the shift toward a greener society. What is owed is an efficient and responsive disaster management system. Accordingly, Congress should elevate the Federal Emergency Management Agency to the status of an independent cabinet agency, granting it authority over federal emergency decisions.[32] It must reconfigure FEMA's statutory mission and operational programs to effectively address long-term social, economic, and environmental risks in hazard-prone regions. Currently, the major payments available to individuals for loss and damage (FEMA's Individual Assistance program) are linked to housing values rather than needs. So wealthy individuals and neighborhoods tend to get bigger slices. People deserve early warning systems that track the progression of an impending extreme event and a safe place to go when that event happens. Transportation, fueled by renewable sources, should be available to get people out of harm's way.

Those who have suffered discrimination need a FEMA that is better coordinated with other federal agencies connected to the federal safety net programs, which offer a target for reparations. If closing the racial wealth gap is a goal and if the country is to protect "life, liberty and the pursuit of happiness," a reparations package that includes federal, state, local, and private corporations and organizations for Black Americans is in order. This package should include individual and collective public benefits that simultaneously builds wealth and eliminates debt among Black citizens.

What is owed is a K–12 curriculum that explores the legacy of discriminatory land use policies, revealing how past racist practices influence present-day environmental injustices in American cities.[33] Geography courses could let students explore the impact of redlining by teaching skills and policy analysis, emphasizing the principle of non-repetition. Students deserve to walk away from a liberal arts curriculum with concrete skills, including those that will help communities adapt to climate change. For instance, students in New Orleans can take engineering courses on how to build a better levee. This curriculum needs to be taught in a well-funded education system that drives resources equitably based on need.

What is owed is health care that separates health insurance from employment, a single-payer system that provides universal care without significant cost sharing. Climate change will increase health care needs. In addition, people who have suffered discrimination deserve to have medical debt eliminated by the federal government.[34] Those who have been injured by discrimination should be shielded from health insurance that is driven by profit, which widens inequities and disproportionately penalizes low-wage essential and frontline workers. Detaching health insurance from employment is a step toward reducing systemic racial, ethnic, and income disparities in health-care access, while also streamlining the system and reducing administrative complexities for employees and employers.

What is owed are civic organizations that will monitor progress toward an area's reparative goals, holding those responsible to concrete metrics and measurable outcomes. Such organizations would monitor conditions of the environment, collect water samples, test levee integrity, survey residents about the impact of climate change, and document local pollution. They would also track the effects of

climate change at a local level, providing virtual and physical feedback through postings in public venues, doctors'
offices, post offices, and grocery stores.

What is owed is the compensation and the programs
that will remedy current hazards that are the result of past
racial injustice.

* * *

REPARATIONS ARE A measure of a country's power dynamic;
their receipt by victims represents formal recognition and
political accountability by the ruling class. Reparations are
not driven by a sudden change of heart or a warm public
conversation. Reparations won't come through a societal
revelation that policies once considered normal are now
recognized as violations of human rights. After all, defense
of the institution of slavery brought the country to fight a
civil war. Instead, reparations will come as a result of the
demands of the victims and their efforts to mobilize alongside allies within the ruling class.

Demanding what is owed organizes people toward
power. When people gain reparations, it does not imply
that they have reached equality. It signals instead that they
understand what they deserve.

NOTES

INTRODUCTION

1. Larry Buchanan, Quoctrung Bui, and Jugal K. Patel, "Black Lives Matter May Be the Largest Movement in U.S. History," *New York Times*, July 3, 2020, https://www.nytimes.com/interactive /2020/07/03/us/george-floyd-protests-crowd-size.html.
2. "Racial Injustice and Corporate Funding | McKinsey," accessed March 27, 2024, ww.mckinsey.com/bem/our-insights/corporate -commitments-to-racial-justice-an-update.
3. "Mapping Police Violence," Campaign Zero, accessed April 16, 2024, https://mappingpoliceviolence.org/.
4. Elizabeth Blair, "Report: Last Year Ended with a Surge in Book Bans," NPR, April 16, 2024, Books, https://www.npr.org/2024 /04/16/1245037718/book-bans-2023-pen-america.
5. Ashley Parker and Toluse Olorunnipa, "Trump 'White Power' Tweet Set Off a Scramble Inside the White House—but No Clear Condemnation," *Washington Post*, June 30, 2020, https://www .washingtonpost.com/politics/trump-white-power-tweet-set-off -a-scramble-inside-the-white-house-but-no-clear-condemnation /2020/06/29/6fd88c2c-ba21-11ea-8cf5-9c1b8d7f84c6_story.html.
6. *Oxford English Dictionary*, s.v. "white supremacy."
7. Kelebogile T. Resane, "White Fragility, White Supremacy and White Normativity Make Theological Dialogue on Race Difficult," *In Die Skriflig* 55, no. 1 (2021): 1–10, https://doi.org/10 .4102/ids.v55i1.2661.

8. Gloria Wekker, *White Innocence: Paradoxes of Colonialism and Race* (Durham, NC: Duke University Press, 2016).

9. Erin Blakemore, "How Dolls Helped Win Brown v. Board of Education," HISTORY, published March 27, 2018, last modified September 29, 2023, https://www.history.com/news/brown -v-board-of-education-doll-experiment.

10. Debra Kamin, "Black Homeowners Face Discrimination in Appraisals," *New York Times*, August 25, 2020, Real Estate, https://www.nytimes.com/2020/08/25/realestate/blacks-minorities -appraisals-discrimination.html.

11. Alexandria Burris, "Indianapolis Homeowner Had a White Friend Stand in for Third Appraisal. Her Home Value Doubled," *Indianapolis Star*, May 13, 2021, https://www.indystar.com /story/money/2021/05/13/indianapolis-black-homeowner -home-appraisal-discrimination-fair-housing-center-central -indiana/4936571001/.

12. Andre M. Perry and Jonathan Rothwell, "The Black Progress Index: Examining the Social Factors That Influence Black Well-Being," Brookings, September 2022, accessed November 4, 2023, https://www.brookings.edu/articles/the black-progress-index/.

13. Na Zhao, "Homeownership Rates by Race and Ethnicity," February 6, 2024, https://eyeonhousing.org/2024/02/homeownership -rates-by-race-and-ethnicity-3/.

14. Amy K. Glasmeier, "New Data Posted: 2023 Living Wage Calculator," Living Wage Institute, February 1, 2023, https://livingwage.mit.edu/articles/103-new-data-posted-2023-living -wage-calculator.

15. Andre M. Perry and Rashawn Ray, "Evanston's Grants to Black Homeowners Aren't Enough. But They Are Reparations," *Washington Post*, April 1, 2021, https://www.washingtonpost.com /outlook/evanston-housing-reparations/2021/04/01/4342833e -9243-11eb-9668-89be11273c09_story.html.

16. A. Kirsten Mullen and William A. Darity Jr., "Evanston, Ill., Approved 'Reparations.' Except It Isn't Reparations," *Washington Post*, March 28, 2021, Opinion, https://www.washingtonpost .com/opinions/2021/03/28/evanston-ill-approved-reparations -housing-program-except-it-isnt-reparations/.

17. Hoang Pham, Imani Nokuri, Fatima Dahir, and Mira Joseph, "Students for Fair Admissions v. Harvard FAQ: Navigating the Evolving Implications of the Court's Ruling," Stanford Law

School, December 12, 2023, https://law.stanford.edu/2023/12/12/students-for-fair-admissions-v-harvard-faq-navigating-the-evolving-implications-of-the-courts-ruling/.

CHAPTER 1: NOT A BUSINESS VENTURE

1. Richard Nixon, Address Accepting the Presidential Nomination at the Republican National Convention, Miami Beach, Florida, August 8, 1968, transcript at American Presidency Project, University of California, Santa Barbara, https://www.presidency.ucsb.edu/documents/address-accepting-the-presidential-nomination-the-republican-national-convention-miami.

2. William Darity Jr., "Why Reparations Are Needed to Close the Racial Wealth Gap," *New York Times*, September 24, 2021, https://www.nytimes.com/2021/09/24/business/reparations-wealth-gap.html.

3. Juliet Michaelson, Sorcha Mahony, and Jonathan Schifferes, *Measuring Well-Being: A Guide for Practitioners* (New Economics Foundation, July 2012), https://neweconomics.org/uploads/files/measuring-wellbeing.pdf.

4. Giovanni Russonello, "Jazz Has Always Been Protest Music. Can It Meet This Moment?" *New York Times*, September 3, 2020, https://www.nytimes.com/2020/09/03/arts/music/jazz-protest-academia.html.

5. Jason L. Riley, *False Black Power* (Conshohocken, PA: Templeton Press, 2017), 22.

6. Ben Nadler and Jeff Amy, "Georgia Gov. Kemp Signs GOP Election Bill Amid an Outcry," Associated Press, March 26, 2021, https://apnews.com/article/donald-trump-legislature-bills-state-elections-voting-rights-b2b014cc81894a50fc513168a5f1d0b8.

CHAPTER 2: POWER TO LIVE

1. "'I've Been to the Mountaintop,'" The Martin Luther King, Jr. Research and Education Institute, accessed June 24, 2024, https://kinginstitute.sites.stanford.edu/ive-been-mountaintop.

2. Elizabeth Arias and Jiaquan Xu, "United States Life Tables, 2019," *National Vital Statistics Reports* 70, no. 19 (2022): 1–59, https://pubmed.ncbi.nlm.nih.gov/35319436/. Throughout this book, terminology for group categories, like Latino and Latinx, reflects the terms used in my sources.

3. Perry and Rothwell, "The Black Progress Index."
4. Romesh Diwan, "Relational Wealth and the Quality of Life," *Journal of Socio-Economics* 29, no. 4 (July 2000): 305–40, https://doi.org/10.1016/S1053-5357(00)00073-1.
5. Raj Chetty, Michael Stepner, Sarah Abraham, Shelby Lin, Benjamin Scuderi, Nicholas Turner, Augustin Bergeron, and David Cutler, "The Association between Income and Life Expectancy in the United States, 2001–2014," *Journal of the American Medical Association* 315, no. 16 (2016): 1750–66, https://doi.org/10.1001/jama.2016.4226.
6. *The Negro Family: The Case for National Action* (US Department of Labor, March 1965), https://www.dol.gov/general/aboutdol/history/webid-moynihan.
7. Yvette C. Cozier et al., "Racism, Segregation, and Risk of Obesity in the Black Women's Health Study," *American Journal of Epidemiology* 179, no. 7 (April 1, 2014): 875–83, https://doi.org/10.1093/aje/kwu004.
8. Alexander Hermann, "In Nearly Every State, People of Color Are Less Likely to Own Homes Compared to White Households," *Housing Perspectives* (blog), Joint Center for Housing Studies, Harvard University, February 8, 2023, https://www.jchs.harvard.edu/blog/nearly-every-state-people-color-are-less-likely-own-homes-compared-white-households.
9. Casey Breen, "The Longevity Benefits of Homeownership," working paper, New Economics Papers, April 15, 2023, https://ideas.repec.org//p/osf/socarx/7ya3f.html.
10. Cheryl Zlotnick, Inbal Manor-Lavon, and Einav Srulovici, "Comparison between Non-Immigrant and 2nd Generation Immigrant Youth: Self-Reported Health Status, BMI, and Internal and External Resources," *Youth & Society* 54, no. 1 (2022): 3–22, https://doi.org/10.1177/0044118X20952663.
11. Anna Zajacova and Elizabeth M. Lawrence, "The Relationship between Education and Health: Reducing Disparities through a Contextual Approach," *Annual Review of Public Health* 39 (April 1, 2018): 273–89, https://doi.org/10.1146/annurev-publhealth-031816-044628.
12. David M. Cutler and Adriana Lleras-Muney, "Understanding Differences in Health Behaviors by Education," *Journal of Health Economics* 29, no. 1 (January 2010): 1–28, https://doi.org/10.1016/j.jhealeco.2009.10.003.

13. Camille Busette et al., "How We Rise: How Social Networks Impact Economic Mobility in Racine, WI, San Francisco, CA, and Washington, DC," Brookings, January 2021, https://www.brookings.edu/wp-content/uploads/2021/01/rpi_20210112_howwerise_racine_sanfran_dc_fullreport.pdf.

14. Sanggon Nam, "The Effects of Religious Attendance and Obesity on Health by Race/Ethnicity," *Osong Public Health and Research Perspectives* 4, no. 2 (April 2013): 81–88, https://doi.org/10.1016/j.phrp.2013.03.002; R. Frank Gillum, "Frequency of Attendance at Religious Services, Overweight, and Obesity in American Women and Men: The Third National Health and Nutrition Examination Survey," *Annals of Epidemiology* 16, no. 9 (September 2006): 655–60, https://doi.org/10.1016/j.annepidem.2005.11.002.

15. Jo Jones and William D. Mosher, "Fathers' Involvement with Their Children: United States, 2006–2010," *National Health Statistics Reports* 71 (December 20, 2013), https://www.cdc.gov/nchs/data/nhsr/nhsr071.pdf.

16. Chadwick L. Menning, "Nonresident Fathers' Involvement and Adolescents' Smoking," *Journal of Health and Social Behavior* 47, no. 1 (March 2006): 32–46, https://doi.org/10.1177/002214650604700103; Paul R. Amato and Joan G. Gilbreth, "Nonresident Fathers and Children's Well-Being: A Meta-Analysis," *Journal of Marriage and the Family* 61, no. 3 (1999): 557–73, https://doi.org/10.2307/353560; Laurence Steinberg, "We Know Some Things: Parent-Adolescent Relationships in Retrospect and Prospect," *Journal of Research on Adolescence* 11, no. 1 (2001): 1–19, https://doi.org/10.1111/1532-7795.00001.

17. Jones and Mosher, "Fathers' Involvement with Their Children."

18. Gretchen Livingston and Kim Parker, "Living Arrangements and Father Involvement," in *A Tale of Two Fathers: More Are Active, but More Are Absent* (Pew Research Center, June 15, 2011), https://www.pewresearch.org/social-trends/2011/06/15/chapter-1-living-arrangements-and-father-involvement/.

19. Armon R. Perry and Mikia Bright, "African American Fathers and Incarceration: Paternal Involvement and Child Outcomes," *Social Work in Public Health* 27, no. 1–2 (2012): 187–203, https://doi.org/10.1080/19371918.2011.629856; Rebekah Levine Coley and Daphne C. Hernandez, "Predictors

of Paternal Involvement for Resident and Nonresident Low-Income Fathers," *Developmental Psychology* 42, no. 6 (November 2006): 1041–56, https:/doi.org/10.1037/0012-1649.42.6.1041.

20. "Most of the World Breathes Unsafe Air, Taking More Than 2 Years Off Global Life Expectancy," Energy Policy Institute of Chicago (EPIC), June 14, 2022, https://epic.uchicago.edu/news/most-of-the-world-breathes-unsafe-air-taking-more-than-2-years-off-global-life-expectancy/.

21. Oliver E. J. Wing, William Lehman, Paul D. Bates, Christopher C. Sampson, Niall Quinn, Andrew M. Smith, Jeffrey C. Neal, Jeremy R. Porter, and Carolyn Kousky, "Inequitable Patterns of US Flood Risk in the Anthropocene," *Nature Climate Change* 12 (2022): 156–62, https://www.nature.com/articles/s41558-021-01265-6; Lorien Nesbitt, Michael J. Meitner, Cynthia Girling, Stephen R. J. Sheppard, and Yuhao Lu, "Who Has Access to Urban Vegetation? A Spatial Analysis of Distributional Green Equity in 10 US Cities," *Landscape and Urban Planning* 181 (January 2019): 51–79, https://doi.org/10.1016/j.landurbplan.2018.08.007.

22. Jeremy Hoffman, Vivek Shandas, and Nicholas Pendleton, "The Effects of Historical Housing Policies on Resident Exposure to Intra-Urban Heat: A Study of 108 US Urban Areas," *Climate* 8, no. 1 (2020), https://doi.org/10.3390/cli8010012.

CHAPTER 3: FORTY ACRES AND A MALL

1. Henry Louis Gates Jr., "The Truth Behind '40 Acres and a Mule,'" *Root* (blog), January 7, 2013, https://www.theroot.com/the-truth-behind-40-acres-and-a-mule-1790894780.

2. Josef C. James, "Sherman at Savannah," *Journal of Negro History* 39, no. 2 (April 1954): 127–37.

3. Sarah McCammon, "The Story Behind '40 Acres and a Mule,'" *All Things Considered*, NPR, January 12, 2015, https://www.npr.org/sections/codeswitch/2015/01/12/376781165/the-story-behind-40-acres-and-a-mule.

4. Andre M. Perry, Jonathan Rothwell, and David Harshbarger, "The Devaluation of Assets in Black Neighborhoods," Brookings, November 27, 2018, https://www.brookings.edu/articles/devaluation-of-assets-in-black-neighborhoods/.

5. "About Us," Citywide Youth Development, https://citywideyouthdevelopment.org/about-us.

6. Andre M. Perry, Jonathan Rothwell, and David Harshbarger, "Five-Star Reviews, One-Star Profits: The Devaluation of Businesses in Black Communities," Brookings, February 18, 2020, https://www.brookings.edu/articles/five-star-reviews-one-star-profits-the-devaluation-of-businesses-in-black-communities/.

7. Mercey Livingston, "These Are the Major Brands Donating to the Black Lives Matter Movement," CNET, June 16, 2020, https://www.cnet.com/culture/companies-donating-black-lives-matter/.

8. Peter Eberhardt, Howard Wial, J. B. Schramm, Derwin Sisnett, and Laura Maher, "Breaking the Glass Bottleneck: The Economic Potential of Black and Hispanic Real Estate Developers and the Constraints They Face," Grove Impact Reports, March 2023, https://reports.groveimpact.org/breaking-the-glass-bottleneck/.

9. Marcus Dieterle, "Video of the Week: History of Edmondson Village Shopping Center," Baltimore Fishbowl, August 12, 2022, https://baltimorefishbowl.com/stories/video-of-the-week-history-of-edmondson-village-shopping-center/.

10. Dieterle, "History of Edmondson Village Shopping Center."

11. "Roof Collapses in Gas-Fueled Fire at Edmondson Village Shopping Center," CBS Baltimore, November 22, 2019, https://www.cbsnews.com/baltimore/news/edmondson-village-shopping-center-fire-west-baltimore/.

12. David Collins and Khiree Stewart, "1 Dead after 5 High School Students Shot at Baltimore Shopping Center," WBAL-TV, January 5, 2023, https://www.wbaltv.com/article/edmondson-village-shopping-center-shooting/42395826.

13. Sherry Karabin, "Crowdfunding Returns as Developers Look for New Sources of Equity," Urban Land, October 6, 2023, https://urbanland.uli.org/development-business/crowdfunding-returns-as-developers-look-for-new-sources-of-equity.

14. Jasmine Vaughn-Hall, "Relaxed Covenant Greenlights Edmondson Village Shopping Center Redevelopment," *Baltimore Banner*, August 11, 2023, https://www.thebaltimorebanner.com/community/edmondson-village-shopping-center-west-baltimore-chicago-trend-IGKCHQPLT5CWJGW7PYBJJPUFHI/.

15. Richard Rothstein, "How Government Policies Cemented the Racism That Reigns in Baltimore," *American Prospect*, April 29, 2015, https://prospect.org/justice/government-policies-cemented -racism-reigns-baltimore/.

16. Jack Watson, "Families Enjoy Holiday Party at Edmondson Village Shopping Center," WMAR2 News, Baltimore, December 8, 2023, https://www.wmar2news.com/local/families-enjoy -holiday-party-at-edmondson-village-shopping-center.

CHAPTER 4: BUSINESS-BUILT BLACK POWER

1. Charles I. Jones, "The Facts of Economic Growth," in *Handbook of Macroeconomics*, vol. 2A, ed. John B. Taylor and Harald Uhlig (Amsterdam: Elsevier, 2016), 3–70; Jonathan Rothwell, Andre M. Perry, and Mike Andrews, "The Black Innovators Who Elevated the United States: Reassessing the Golden Age of Invention," Brookings, November 23, 2020, https://www .brookings.edu/articles/the-black-innovators-who-elevated-the -united-states-reassessing-the-golden-age-of-invention/.

2. Encyclopedia.com, s.v., "Slave Entrepreneurs."

3. Catherine Thorbecke, "US Economy 'Has Never Worked Fairly for Black Americans,' Treasury Chief Says," ABCNews, January 17, 2022, https://abcnews.go.com/Business/treasury-secretary-us -economy-worked-fairly-black-americans/story?id=82308011.

4. Calculated using the census-defined category, "Black alone or in combination with one or more other races."

5. Andre M. Perry, Manann Donoghoe, and Hannah Stephens, "Closing the Black Employer Gap: Insights from the Latest Data on Black-Owned Businesses," Brookings, February 15, 2024, https://www.brookings.edu/articles/closing-the-black-employer -gap-insights-from-the-latest-data-on-black-owned-businesses/.

6. Jonathan Rothwell, "Employing Others Is Linked to Wealth and Wellbeing," Gallup, April 11, 2024, https://news.gallup.com /poll/643268/employing-others-linked-wealth-wellbeing.aspx.

7. Alina Schnake-Mahl, Jessica A. R. Williams, Barry Keppard, and Mariana Arcaya, "A Public Health Perspective on Small Business Development: A Review of the Literature," *Journal of Urbanism: International Research on Placemaking and Urban Sustainability* 11, no. 4 (2018), https://doi.org/10.1080/17549175.2018.1461678.

8. Craig Evan Pollack, Sekai Chideya, Catherine Cubbin, Brie Williams, Mercedes Dekker, and Paula Braveman, "Should

Health Studies Measure Wealth? A Systematic Review," *American Journal of Preventive Medicine* 33, no. 3 (September 2007): 250–64.

9. Cheryl Baehr, "Bait Stuns with an Upscale Approach to Seafood," *Riverfront Times* (St. Louis), September 4, 2019, https://www.riverfronttimes.com/food-drink/bait-stuns-with-an-upscale-approach-to-seafood-32211977.

10. "Bridging the Startup Funding Gap for Women, Black and Latinx Entrepreneurs," Olin Brookings Commission, 2023, https://olin.wustl.edu/_assets/docs/research/OlinBrookingsCommission2023-PolicyPaper.pdf.

11. Homepage, Path to 15|55, https://www.pathto1555.org/.

12. Dag Detter and Stefan Fölster, *The Public Wealth of Cities: How to Unlock Hidden Assets to Boost Growth and Prosperity* (Washington, DC: Brookings Institution Press, 2017).

13. Andre M. Perry and Carl Romer, "To Expand the Economy, Invest in Black Businesses," Brookings, December 31, 2020, https://www.brookings.edu/articles/to-expand-the-economy-invest-in-black-businesses/.

CHAPTER 5: GETTING TO CLOSING

1. Bradford Tuckfield, "What Home Ownership Has to Do with Healthy Families," Institute for Family Studies, November 28, 2022, https://ifstudies.org/blog/what-home-ownership-has-to-do-with-healthy-families; Breen, "Longevity Benefits of Homeownership."

2. Rachel Bogardus Drew, "Believing in Homeownership: Where Does the American Dream Idea Come From?," Shelterforce, August 20, 2014, https://shelterforce.org/2014/08/20/believing_in_homeownership_where_does_the_american_dream_idea_come_from/.

3. J. H. Cullum Clark, "The Benefits of Homeownership Mean We Should Still Believe in the American Dream," *Catalyst*, no. 12 (Fall 2018), https://www.bushcenter.org/catalyst/opportunity-road/clark-benefits-of-home-ownership.

4. Barack Obama, "Remarks by the President on Responsible Homeownership," White House, Office of the Press Secretary, August 6, 2013, https://obamawhitehouse.archives.gov/the-press-office/2013/08/06/remarks-president-responsible-home ownership.

5. "Racial Differences in Economic Security: Housing," US Department of the Treasury, Office of Economic Policy, November 4, 2022, https://home.treasury.gov/news/featured -stories/racial-differences-in-economic-security-housing.

6. Andre M. Perry and David Harshbarger, "America's Formerly Redlined Neighborhoods Have Changed, and So Must Solutions to Rectify Them," Brookings, October 14, 2019, https://www.brookings.edu/research/americas-formerly-redlined -areas-changed-so-must-solutions/.

7. Perry, Rothwell, and Harshbarger, "Devaluation of Assets in Black Neighborhoods."

8. Andre M. Perry, Hannah Stephens, and Manann Donoghoe, "Black Wealth Is Increasing, but so Is the Racial Wealth Gap," Brookings, January 9, 2024, https://www.brookings.edu/arti cles/black-wealth-is-increasing-but-so-is-the-racial-wealth -gap/.

9. "Gap between Black and White Renting Families Who Could Afford a Mortgage Narrowed Significantly during the Pandemic," Zillow press release, February 23, 2024, https://zillow.mediaroom .com/2024-02-23-Gap-between-Black-and-white-renting -families-who-could-afford-a-mortgage-narrowed-significantly -during-the-pandemic.

10. Jarrell Dillard and Jonnelle Marte, "Housing Affordability Near Record Lows Hits Black Buyers Particularly Hard," *Bloomberg*, January 29, 2024, https://www.bloomberg.com/news/articles /2024-01-29/housing-affordability-crisis-hits-us-black-buyers -particularly-hard.

11. "'The Color of Law' Details How U.S. Housing Policies Created Segregation," NPR, May 17, 2017, https://www.npr.org /2017/05/17/528822128/the-color-of-law-details-how-u-s -housing-policies-created-segregation.

12. Benjamin Harris and Sydney Schreiner Wertz, "Racial Differences in Economic Security: The Racial Wealth Gap," US Department of the Treasury, September 15, 2022, https://home .treasury.gov/news/featured-stories/racial-differences-economic -security-racial-wealth-gap.

13. Aniket Mehrota, Daniel Pang, Jun Zhu, Jung Hyun Choi, and Janneke Ratcliffe, "Evidence of Disparities in Access to Mortgage Credit," Urban Institute, March 2024, in "History & Background Presentation by NFHA—SPCP Toolkit for

Mortgage Lenders," Special Purpose Credit Programs, accessed March 9, 2024, https://spcptoolkit.com/history-background -presentation-by-nfha/.

14. Casey Tolan, Audrey Ash, and Rene Marsh, "The Nation's Largest Credit Union Rejected More Than Half Its Black Conventional Mortgage Applicants," CNN Business, December 14, 2023, https://www.cnn.com/2023/12/14/business/navy-federal-credit -union-black-applicants-invs/index.html.

15. Rene Marsh, Casey Tolan, and Audrey Ash, "Class Action Lawsuit Alleging Discrimination Filed against Navy Federal after CNN Exclusive Report," CNN Business, December 18, 2023, https://www.cnn.com/2023/12/18/business/class-action -lawsuit-navy-federal-invs/index.html.

16. Tolan, Ash, and Marsh, "Nation's Largest Credit Union Rejected More than Half."

17. Lisa Rice and Deidre Swesnik, "Discriminatory Effects of Credit Scoring on Communities of Color," National Fair Housing Alliance, Symposium on Credit Scoring and Credit Reporting, Suffolk University Law School and National Consumer Law Center, June 6–7, 2012, https://nationalfairhousing .org/resource/discriminatory-effects-of-credit-scoring-on -communities-of-color/.

18. "§1002.8 Special Purpose Credit Programs," Consumer Financial Protection Bureau, accessed March 3, 2024, https://www .consumerfinance.gov/rules-policy/regulations/1002/8/.

19. Rob Wile, "Bank of America Announces Zero Down Payment, Zero Closing Cost Mortgages for First-Time Homebuyers in Black and Hispanic Communities Nationwide," NBC News, August 31, 2022, https://www.nbcnews.com/business /consumer/bank-america-zero-down-payment-mortgage-first -time-buyers-details-rcna45662.

20. "SPCP Toolkit for Mortgage Lenders," Special Purpose Credit Programs.

21. Jung Hyun Choi and Peter J. Mattingly, "What Different Denial Rates Can Tell Us about Racial Disparities in the Mortgage Market," Urban Institute, January 13, 2022, https://www .urban.org/urban-wire/what-different-denial-rates-can-tell-us -about-racial-disparities-mortgage-market.

22. Laurie Goodman and Jun Zhu, "The Future of Headship and Homeownership," Urban Institute, January 21, 2021,

https://www.urban.org/research/publication/future-headship
-and-homeownership.

23. Rakesh Kochhar and Mohamad Moslimani, "1. Wealth Gaps
within Racial and Ethnic Groups," Pew Research Center,
December 4, 2023, https://www.pewresearch.org/race-ethnicity
/2023/12/04/wealth-gaps-within-racial-and-ethnic-groups/.

24. Mortgage Rates, Forbes Advisor, accessed June 6, 2024, https://
www.forbes.com/advisor/mortgages/mortgage-rates/.

25. "Record-High Prices and Record-Low Inventory Make It
Increasingly Difficult to Achieve Homeownership, Particularly for Black Americans," National Association of Realtors,
February 4, 2022, https://www.nar.realtor/newsroom/record
-high-prices-and-record-low-inventory-make-it-increasingly
-difficult-to-achieve-homeownership-particularly-for-black
-americans.

26. "Whole Blocks, Whole City: Reclaiming Vacant Property
throughout Baltimore," Abell Foundation, February 2023, https://
abell.org/publication/reclaiming-vacant-property/.

27. Victoria Méndez, "What Is Mutual Aid, and How Can It Transform Our World?" Global Giving, February 3, 2022, https://
www.globalgiving.org/learn/what-is-mutual-aid/.

28. Dan Kildee and Amy Hovey, "Land Banking 101: What Is a
Land Bank?" US Department of Housing and Urban Development, Neighborhood Stabilization Program, accessed June
6, 2024, https://files.hudexchange.info/resources/documents
/LandBankingBasics.pdf.

29. "Equitable Development Company Parity Wins $25,000 Prize
at Social Innovation Lab Impact Forum," Johns Hopkins Technology Ventures, June 12, 2020, https://ventures.jhu.edu/news
/parity-social-innovation-lab-cohort-prize-housing/.

30. "Baltimore Receives $20 Million for Economic Mobility and
Housing Equity," Baltimore City press release, Mayor Brandon
M. Scott, January 26, 2022, https://mayor.baltimorecity.gov
/news/press-releases/2022-01-26-baltimore-receives-20-million
-economic-mobility-and-housing-equity.

31. "Our Mission," Ignite Capital, accessed March 10, 2024, https:
//www.ignitecapital.org.

32. Tracy Hadden Loh and Hanna Love, "The Emerging Solidarity
Economy: A Primer on Community Ownership of Real Estate,"
Brookings, July 19, 2021, https://www.brookings.edu/articles

/the-emerging-solidarity-economy-a-primer-on-community
-ownership-of-real-estate/.

33. Loh and Love, "Emerging Solidarity Economy."
34. "NAREB Sets Goal of 2 Million New Black Home Owners,"
National Association of Real Estate Brokers press release, July
22, 2018, https://www.nareb.com/press/nareb-sets-goal-of-2
-million-new-black-home-owners-2/.

CHAPTER 6: MARRIAGE MATERIAL

1. Hearing on "Building a Strong Foundation: Investments Today
for a More Competitive Tomorrow," Before the Joint Economic Committee, 117th Congress, April 27, 2022 (testimony
of Michelle Holder, president and CEO of Washington Center for Equitable Growth), https://www.jec.senate.gov/public
/_cache/files/4ae1ef7e-55e7-4bb0-a05d-a3280280ce15/holder
-joint-economic-committee-building-on-a-strong-foundation
-testimony.pdf.
2. Chanell Washington and Laquitta Walker, "District of Colum-
bia Had Lowest Percentage of Married Black Adults in 2015–
2019," Marriage Prevalence for Black Adults Varies by State,
Bureau of the Census, July 19, 2022, https://www.census.gov
/library/stories/2022/07/marriage-prevalence-for-black-adults
-varies-by-state.html.
3. Robert Staples, "Changes in Black Family Structure: The Conflict between Family Ideology and Structural Conditions,"
Journal of Marriage and Family 47, no. 4 (November 1985):
1005–13.
4. Daniel Schneider, "Wealth and the Marital Divide," *American Journal of Sociology* 117, no. 2 (September 2011): 627–67,
https://doi.org/10.1086/661594.
5. Valerie Kincade Oppenheimer, "A Theory of Marriage Timing,"
American Journal of Sociology 94, no. 3 (November 1998): 563–
91; Andrew J. Cherlin, *The Marriage-Go-Round: The State of
Marriage and the Family in America Today* (New York: Knopf,
2010); Daniel T. Lichter and Zhenchao Qian, "Serial Cohabitation and the Marital Life Course," *Journal of Marriage and
Family* 70, no. 4 (2008): 861–78, https://doi.org/10.1111/j
.1741-3737.2008.00532.x.
6. Schneider, "Wealth and the Marital Divide."
7. Schneider, "Wealth and the Marital Divide."

8. Alicia Eads and Laura Tach, "Wealth and Inequality in the Stability of Romantic Relationships," in "Wealth Inequality: Economic and Social Dimensions," special issue, *RSF: The Russell Sage Foundation Journal of the Social Sciences* 2, no. 6 (October 2016): 197–224, https://doi.org/10.7758/rsf.2016.2.6.10.

9. Brad Wilcox, "Two Is Wealthier Than One," American Enterprise Institute, October 7, 2021, https://www.aei.org/research -products/report/two-is-wealthier-than-one/.

10. Fenaba R. Addo and Daniel T. Lichter, "Marriage, Marital History, and Black–White Wealth Differentials among Older Women," *Journal of Marriage and Family* 75, no. 2 (April 2013): 342–62, http://www.jstor.org/stable/23440786.

11. "What Are Marriage Penalties and Bonuses?" Tax Center Briefing Book, https://www.taxpolicycenter.org/briefing-book/what -are-marriage-penalties-and-bonuses.

12. Adam Looney and Nicholas Turner, "Work and Opportunity Before and After Incarceration," Brookings, March 2018, https://www.brookings.edu/wp-content/uploads/2018/03/es _20180314_looneyincarceration_final.pdf.

CHAPTER 7: THE COMMUNITY AS A GOOD SCHOOL

1. "Adult Education," Louisiana Department of Public Safety and Corrections, accessed March 16, 2024, https://doc.louisiana.gov /public-programs-resources/return-for-good/adulteducation/.

2. Voice of the Inexperienced, Redistricting Data Hub (Spencer Nelson and Peter Horton), and the Prison Policy Initiative, "Where People in Prison Come From: The Geography of Mass Incarceration in Louisiana," Prison Policy Initiative press release, July 2023, https://www.prisonpolicy.org/origin/la/2022/report.html.

3. Michael J. Waguespack, "Student Racial Demographics: Louisiana Elementary and Secondary Public and Private Schools," informational brief, Louisiana Legislative Auditor, January 25, 2023, https://app.lla.state.la.us/publicreports.nsf/0/a4fa835e5 738df42862589420071c04c/$file/00000951.pdf?openelement &.7773098.

4. Wesley Muller, "Another Study Links Poverty to Poor Results at Louisiana Schools," *Louisiana Illuminator*, January 31, 2023, https://lailluminator.com/2023/01/31/another-study-links -poverty-to-poor-results-at-louisiana-schools/.

5. Cassie Burke, "Why Is Education Important? The Power of an Educated Society," Unity Environmental University, October 4, 2023, https://unity.edu/articles/why-education-is-important/.

6. Margaret diZerega and George Chochos, "Postsecondary Education in Prison Is a Racial Equity Strategy," Vera Institute of Justice, July 14, 2020, https://www.vera.org/news/target-2020 /postsecondary-education-in-prison-is-a-racial-equity-strategy.

7. Leila Morsy and Richard Rothstein, "Mass Incarceration and Children's Outcomes: Criminal Justice Policy Is Education Policy," Economic Policy Institute, December 15, 2016, https:// www.epi.org/publication/mass-incarceration-and-childrens -outcomes/.

8. David M. Cutler and Adriana Lleras-Muney, "Understanding Differences in Health Behaviors by Education," *Journal of Health Economics* 29, no. 1 (2010): 1–28.

9. Cutler and Lleras-Muney, "Understanding Differences in Health Behaviors by Education."

10. William R. Emmons and Lowell R. Ricketts, "Unequal Degrees of Affluence: Racial and Ethnic Wealth Differences across Education Levels," Federal Reserve Bank of St. Louis, October 12, 2016, https://www.stlouisfed.org/publications/regional -economist/october-2016/unequal-degrees-of-affluence-racial -and-ethnic-wealth-differences-across-education-levels.

11. "NAEP Mathematics: National Achievement-Level Results," National Assessment of Education Progress, accessed March 14, 2024, https://www.nationsreportcard.gov/mathematics/nation /achievement/?grade=8.

12. Raj Chetty, John Friedman, Emmanuel Saez, Nicholas Turner, and Danny Yagan, "Mobility Report Cards: Income Segregation and Intergenerational Mobility across Colleges in the United States," Opportunity Insights, February 12, 2020, https:// opportunityinsights.org/paper/undermatching/.

13. Krista Mattern, Justine Radunzel, and Matt Harmston, "ACT Composite Score by Family Income," ACT Research & Policy, August 2016, chrome-extension://efaidnbmnnnibpcajpcglclefind mkaj/https://www.act.org/content/dam/act/unsecured/docu ments/R1604-ACT-Composite-Score-by-Family-Income.pdf.

14. "Education," Confronting Anti-Black Racism Resource, Harvard Library, accessed March 13, 2024, https://library.harvard .edu/confronting-anti-black-racism/education.

15. Beth Hawkins, "Wealthier and Whiter: Louisiana School District Secession Gets a Major Boost," *The 74*, May 1, 2024, https://www.the74million.org/article/wealthier-and-whiter-louisiana-school-district-secession-gets-a-major-boost/.

16. Kendra Taylor, Erica Frankenberg, and Genevieve Siegel-Hawley, "Racial Segregation in the Southern Schools, School Districts, and Counties Where Districts Have Seceded," *AERA Open* 5, no. 3 (July 2019), https://doi.org/10.1177/2332858419860152; P. R. Lockhart, "Smaller Communities Are 'Seceding' from Larger School Districts. It's Accelerating School Segregation," *Vox*, September 6, 2019, https://www.vox.com/2019/9/6/20853091/school-secession-racial-segregation-louisiana-alabama?sfns=mo.

17. "K–12 Education: Student Population Has Significantly Diversified, but Many Schools Remain Divided along Racial, Ethnic, and Economic Lines," US Government Accountability Office, July 14, 2022, https://www.gao.gov/products/gao-22-104737.

18. "Secretaries of Education, Agriculture Call on Governors to Equitably Fund Land-Grant HBCUs," US Department of Education press release, September 18, 2023, https://www.ed.gov/news/press-releases/secretaries-education-agriculture-call-governors-equitably-fund-land-grant-hbcus; Katherine Knott, "States Underfunded Historically Black Land Grants by $13 Billion over 3 Decades," Inside Higher Ed, September 20, 2023, https://www.insidehighered.com/news/government/2023/09/20/states-underfunded-black-land-grants-13b-over-30-years.

19. Dignity and Nondiscrimination in Public Education, Idaho statute 33-138, 2021, https://legislature.idaho.gov/statutesrules/idstat/title33/t33ch1/sect33-138/.

20. Sarah Schwartz, "Map: Where Critical Race Theory Is Under Attack," *Education Week*, August 28, 2024, https://www.edweek.org/policy-politics/map-where-critical-race-theory-is-under-attack/2021/06.

21. Nicole Chavez, "Florida Board of Education Approves New Black History Standards That Critics Call 'a Big Step Backward,'" CNN, July 20, 2023, https://www.cnn.com/2023/07/20/us/florida-black-history-education-standards-reaj/index.html.

22. Brenda Álvarez, "Florida's New History Standard: 'A Blow to Our Students and Nation,'" National Education Association, August 3, 2023, https://www.nea.org/nea-today/all-news-articles/floridas-new-history-standard-blow-our-students-and-nation.

23. "NAACP Condemns Gov. DeSantis' Decision to Reject AP Course on African American Studies," NAACP press release, January 20, 2023, https://naacp.org/articles/naacp-condemns -gov-desantis-decision-reject-ap-course-african-american -studies.

24. Char Adams, Allan Smith, and Aadit Tambe, "Map: See Which States Have Passed Critical Race Theory Bills," NBC News, June 17, 2021, https://www.nbcnews.com/news/nbcblk/map-see -which-states-have-passed-critical-race-theory-bills-n1271215.

25. "PEN America Index of School Book Bans—2022–2023," PEN America, https://pen.org/2023-banned-book-list/.

26. Ahmed Ali (@DrAhmednurAli), "If Black children are old enough to experience racism, then other children are old enough to learn about critical race theory," Twitter, May 5, 2021, https: //twitter.com/DrAhmednurAli/status/1389990503270293504.

27. Brooke Migdon and Cheyanne M. Daniels, "DeSantis Sparks Outrage with Rejection of African American Studies Class," The Hill, January 20, 2023, https://thehill.com/homenews /campaign/3821500-desantis-sparks-outrage-with-rejection-of -african-american-studies-class/.

28. Kim Singletary, "Captain New Orleans," *Biz New Orleans*, August 1, 2022, https://www.bizneworleans.com/captain-new -orleans/.

29. "Development Projects by Anthony and Calvin Mackie Will Bring Economic Boom to New Orleans East," STEM NOLA, March 18, 2022, https://stemnola.com/development-projects -by-anthony-and-calvin-mackie-will-bring-economic-boom-to -new-orleans-east/.

30. Rich Collins, "Hollywood Star Anthony Mackie Planning Film Studio in New Orleans East," *Biz New Orleans*, March 17, 2022, https://www.bizneworleans.com/hollywood-star-anthony -mackie-planning-film-studio-in-new-orleans-east/.

31. "Citing the Lack of Diversity in STEM, SGA Founder Dr. Calvin Mackie Calls for a New Approach to Advance STEM Education," FOX4, May 2, 2023, https://fox4kc.com/business /press-releases/ein-presswire/631406494/citing-the-lack-of -diversity-in-stem-sga-founder-dr-calvin-mackie-calls-for-a -new-approach-to-advance-stem-education/.

32. "Provide Expanded Learning Time," Learning Policy Institute, Restarting and Reinventing School, accessed March 16, 2024,

https://restart-reinvent.learningpolicyinstitute.org/provide-expanded-learning-time.

33. "The Transformative Potential of Tutoring for Pre K–12 Learning Outcomes: Lessons from Randomized Evaluations," Abdul Latif Jameel Poverty Action Lab (J-PAL), September 16, 2020, https://www.povertyactionlab.org/publication/transformative-potential-tutoring-pre-k-12-learning-outcomes-lessons-randomized.

34. Ed Trust and MDRC, "The Importance of Strong Relationships between Teachers & Students: A Strategy to Solve Unfinished Learning," The Education Trust, March 17, 2021, https://edtrust.org/resource/the-importance-of-strong-relationships/.

35. "Transformative Potential of Tutoring for Pre K–12 Learning Outcomes."

CHAPTER 8: EMPOWERMENT THROUGH UNITY

1. "Big Three Picket Chants," Unite All Workers for Democracy, https://uawd.org/chants/.

2. Keith Brower Brown, Luis Feliz Leon, and Jane Slaughter, "'No Justice, No Jeeps!' Scenes from the Auto Workers Strike," Labor Notes, September 15, 2023, https://www.labornotes.org/2023/09/no-justice-no-jeeps-scenes-auto-workers-strike.

3. Gabrielle Coppola, David Welch, and Keith Naughton, "What's at Stake as US Autoworkers Threaten to Strike," *Washington Post*, September 14, 2023, https://www.washingtonpost.com/business/2023/09/14/what-s-at-stake-if-uaw-autoworkers-strike-impact-on-gm-explained/7d656c30-5301-11ee-accf-88c266213aac_story.html.

4. Coppola, Welch, and Naughton, "What's at Stake as US Autoworkers Threaten to Strike."

5. Adam S. Hersh, "UAW-Automakers Negotiations Pit Falling Wages against Skyrocketing CEO Pay," *Working Economics* (blog), Economic Policy Institute, September 12, 2023, https://www.epi.org/blog/uaw-automakers-negotiations/.

6. Andre M. Perry, "Black Incomes Outpace the National Average in 124 Majority-Black Cities: So Where's the Investment?" Brookings, November 15, 2017, https://www.brookings.edu/articles/black-incomes-outpace-the-national-average-in-124-majority-black-cities-so-wheres-the-investment/.

7. Lynn Stout, "Corporations Don't Have to Maximize Profits," *New York Times*, April 16, 2015, Opinion, https://www.nytimes .com/roomfordebate/2015/04/16/what-are-corporations -obligations-to-shareholders/corporations-dont-have-to -maximize-profits.

8. Vinson Cunningham, "The Argument of 'Afropessimism,'" *New Yorker*, July 13, 2020, https://www.newyorker.com/magazine /2020/07/20/the-argument-of-afropessimism.

9. Cunningham, "Argument of 'Afropessimism.'"

10. Heidi Shierholz, Margaret Poydock, and Celine McNicholas, "Unionization Increased by 200,000 in 2022," Economic Policy Institute, January 19, 2023, https://www.epi.org/publication /unionization-2022/.

11. Tom Krishner, "Ford and Stellantis Workers Join Those at GM in Approving Contract Settlement That Ended UAW Strikes," AP, Yahoo! Finance, November 18, 2023, https://finance.yahoo.com /news/ford-workers-join-those-gm-061603959.html.

12. "Inside the Fight to Unionize an Amazon Facility in Alabama," YouTube video, 9:11, posted by VICE News, March 17, 2021, https://www.youtube.com/watch?v=zDeXXQZsups.

13. Andre M. Perry, Molly Kinder, Laura Stateler, and Carl Romer, "Amazon's Union Battle in Bessemer, Alabama, Is about Dignity, Racial Justice, and the Future of the American Worker," Brookings, March 16, 2021, https://www.brookings.edu/articles /the-amazon-union-battle-in-bessemer-is-about-dignity-racial -justice-and-the-future-of-the-american-worker/.

14. Megan Armstrong, Eathyn Edwards, and Duwain Pinder, "Corporate Commitments to Racial Justice: An Update," McKinsey Institute for Black Economic Mobility, February 21, 2023, https: //www.mckinsey.com/bem/our-insights/corporate-commitments -to-racial-justice-an-update.

15. Buchanan, Bui, and Patel, "Black Lives Matter May Be the Largest Movement in U.S. History."

16. Chandra Childers, "Rooted in Racism and Economic Exploitation: The Failed Southern Economic Development Model," Economic Policy Institute, October 11, 2023, https://www.epi .org/publication/rooted-in-racism/.

17. "Union Members—2023," US Bureau of Labor Statistics press release, January 23, 2024, https://www.bls.gov/news.release/pdf /union2.pdf.

18. Annie Palmer, "How Amazon Keeps a Close Eye on Employee Activism to Head off Unions," CNBC, October 24, 2020, https://www.cnbc.com/2020/10/24/how-amazon-prevents-unions-by-surveilling-employee-activism.html.

19. Steven Greenhouse, "'Old-School Union Busting': How US Corporations Are Quashing the New Wave of Organizing," *Guardian*, February 26, 2023, https://www.theguardian.com/us-news/2023/feb/26/amazon-trader-joes-starbucks-anti-union-measures.

20. Luis Feliz Leon, "Warehouse Workers Wage Historic Fight for Union Recognition at Amazon," *American Prospect*, February 6, 2021, https://prospect.org/labor/warehouse-workers-wage-historic-fight-for-union-recognition-amazon/.

21. Adie Tomer and Joseph W. Kane, "To Protect Frontline Workers During and After COVID-19, We Must Define Who They Are," Brookings, June 10, 2020, https://www.brookings.edu/articles/to-protect-frontline-workers-during-and-after-covid-19-we-must-define-who-they-are/.

22. Tomer and Kane, "To Protect Frontline Workers."

23. Molly Kinder and Tiffany N. Ford, "Black Essential Workers' Lives Matter. They Deserve Real Change, Not Just Lip Service," Brookings, June 24, 2020, https://www.brookings.edu/articles/black-essential-workers-lives-matter-they-deserve-real-change-not-just-lip-service/.

24. Martin Luther King Jr., "The 50th Anniversary of Martin Luther King, Jr.'s 'All Labor Has Dignity,'" March 18, 2018, https://www.beaconbroadside.com/broadside/2018/03/the-50th-anniversary-of-martin-luther-king-jrs-all-labor-has-dignity.html.

25. Glasmeier, "Living Wage Calculator."

26. Glasmeier, "Living Wage Calculator."

27. Karen Weise and Michael Corkery, "Amazon Workers Vote Down Union Drive at Alabama Warehouse," *New York Times*, April 9, 2021, https://www.nytimes.com/2021/04/09/technology/amazon-defeats-union.html.

28. Andrea Hsu, "Do-Over Union Election at Amazon's Bessemer Warehouse Is Too Close to Call," Alabama Public Radio, March 31, 2022, https://www.apr.org/business-education/2022-03-31/do-over-union-election-at-amazons-bessemer-warehouse-is-too-close-to-call.

29. "Region 10-Atlanta Announces Results of Bessemer Amazon Ballot Count," National Labor Relations Board press release,

March 31, 2022, https://www.nlrb.gov/news-outreach/region
-10-atlanta/region-10-atlanta-announces-results-of-bessemer
-amazon-ballot-count; Alina Selyukh, "Amazon Warehouse
Workers in Alabama Might Get a Third Try at Unionizing," NPR,
April 25, 2024, https://www.npr.org/2024/04/25/1246423390
/amazon-warehouse-alabama-union-vote.

30. Brown, Leon, and Slaughter, "'No Justice, No Jeeps!' Scenes
from the Auto Workers Strike."

CHAPTER 9: REPARATIONS GO TO DC

1. Lucio Vasquez and Katie Watkins, "City of Houston Announces
Plans to Start Moving Fifth Ward Residents Living Near the
Contaminated Union Pacific Railyard," Houston Public Media,
July 13, 2023, https://www.houstonpublicmedia.org/articles
/news/energy-environment/2023/07/13/456833/how-many
-more-people-must-be-diagnosed-with-cancer-city-of-houston
-announces-plans-to-start-moving-fifth-ward-residents-living
-near-the-contaminated-union-pacific-railyard/.

2. Sara Willa Ernst, "'We Know What We Want': 5th Ward Residents Demand Action after Another Confirmed Cancer Cluster," Houston Public Media, February 3, 2021, https://www
.houstonpublicmedia.org/articles/news/health-science/2021
/02/03/390571/5th-ward-cancer-cluster-houston-confirmed/.

3. Rosie Nguyen, "City of Houston Approves $5 Million to
Help Residents Voluntarily Move Out of 'Cancer Clusters,'"
ABC13, September 27, 2023, https://abc13.com/cancer-causing
-chemicals-in-houston-neighborhood-fifth-ward-kashmere
-gardens-union-pacific-creosote-plume/13836280/.

4. Brittany Taylor, "Mayor Turner, HHD Announce Plan to Relocate Houston Residents Away from Contaminated Site," Click-
2Houston, July 13, 2023, https://www.click2houston.com
/news/local/2023/07/13/live-mayor-turner-hhd-announce-new
-developments-to-union-pacific-railroad-contaminated-site/.

5. Andre M. Perry and Jordan Fields, "Boston Task Force on
Reparations Is Setting a Precedent for Other States to Follow,"
Boston Globe, July 28, 2023, https://www.bostonglobe.com
/2023/07/28/opinion/bostons-reparations-task-force-is-setting
-precedent-other-states-follow.

6. Mullen and Darity, "Evanston, Ill., Approved 'Reparations.'
Except It Isn't Reparations."

7. Beatrice Peterson, "Rep. Cori Bush Says $14 Trillion Reparations Bill Will 'Eliminate the Racial Wealth Gap,'" ABC News, March 19, 2023, https://abcnews.go.com/Politics/rep-cori-bush -14-trillion-reparations-bill-eliminate/story?id=99390652.

8. United Nations, United Nations Charter (full text), https:// www.un.org/en/about-us/un-charter/full-text.

9. UN General Assembly, Resolution 60/147, Basic Principles and Guidelines on the Right to a Remedy and Reparation for Victims of Gross Violations of International Human Rights Law and Serious Violations of International Humanitarian Law, https://www.ohchr.org/en/instruments-mechanisms/instruments/basic -principles-and-guidelines-right-remedy-and-reparation.

10. UN General Assembly, Basic Principles on the Right to a Remedy and Reparation.

11. "Brownfield Overview and Definition," US Environmental Protection Agency, https://19january2017snapshot.epa.gov /brownfields/brownfield-overview-and-definition_.html.

12. "About Human Rights and the Environment," United Nations Special Rapporteur on Human Rights and the Environment, https://www.ohchr.org/en/special-procedures/sr-environment /about-human-rights-and-environment.

13. Walter Johnson, "King Cotton's Long Shadow," *Great Divide* (blog), *New York Times*, March 30, 2013, https://archive .nytimes.com/opinionator.blogs.nytimes.com/2013/03/30 /king-cottons-long-shadow/.

14. "Sacrifice Zones," ProPublica, November 2, 2021, https://www .propublica.org/series/sacrifice-zones.

15. Ashley Brown, "City of Houston Offers Relocation for Homeowners, Renters in Fifth Ward Cancer Cluster Areas," Houston Public Media, November 20, 2023, https://www .houstonpublicmedia.org/articles/housing/2023/11/20 /470142/city-provides-update-on-the-relocation-program -residnets-living-near-contaminated-site/.

16. Mullen and Darity, "Evanston, Ill., Approved 'Reparations.' Except It Isn't Reparations."

17. Vasquez and Watkins, "City of Houston Announces Plans to Start Moving Fifth Ward Residents."

18. Pooja Lodhia, "Program Would Relocate 5th Ward and Kashmere Gardens Residents from Cancer Cluster," ABC13, July 13,

2023, https://abc13.com/fifth-ward-kashmere-gardens-cancer-cluster-moving-residents-out-of/13499619/.

19. US EPA Region 5 Brownfields Team, "EPA Brownfields in Detroit and Southeast Michigan," US Environmental Protection Agency, https://storymaps.arcgis.com/stories/05c92d897e684f0991562a0881cb162a.

20. Thomas J. Sugrue, "Motor City: The Story of Detroit," Gilder Lehrman Institute of American History, 2007.

21. "African American Workers at Ford Motor Company," *Archive Insight* (blog), Henry Ford, https://www.thehenryford.org/explore/blog/african-american-workers-at-ford-motor-company/.

22. Joyce Shaw Peterson, "Black Automobile Workers in Detroit, 1910–1930," *Journal of Negro History* 64, no. 3 (1979): 177–90, https://doi.org/10.2307/2717031; Nathaniel Meyersohn, "The Future of the Auto Industry Will Have an Outsized Impact on Black America | CNN Business," CNN, October 7, 2023, https://www.cnn.com/2023/10/07/business/black-workers-auto-industry-uaw-strike/index.html.

23. Christopher L. Foote, Warren C. Whatley, and Gavin Wright, "Arbitraging a Discriminatory Labor Market: Black Workers at the Ford Motor Company, 1918–1947," *Journal of Labor Economics* 21, no. 3 (July 2003): 493–532, https://doi.org/10.1086/374957.

24. Peterson, "Black Automobile Workers in Detroit, 1910–1930."

25. Abas Shkembi, Lauren M. Smith, and Richard L. Neitzel, "Linking Environmental Injustices in Detroit, MI to Institutional Racial Segregation through Historical Federal Redlining," *Journal of Exposure Science & Environmental Epidemiology* (2022), https://doi.org/10.1038/s41370-022-00512-y.

26. *State of the Air*, American Lung Association, 2022, https://www.lung.org/getmedia/74b3d3d3-88d1-4335-95d8-c4e47d0282c1/sota-2022.pdf.

27. Samuel Robinson, "Air Quality Concern Could Become the New Normal," Axios Detroit, July 13, 2023, https://www.axios.com/local/detroit/2023/07/13/air-quality-concern-new-normal-detroit-wildfires.

28. "Reduce Urban Heat Island Effect," US Environmental Protection Agency, https://www.epa.gov/green-infrastructure/reduce-urban-heat-island-effect.

29. Andrew Chee Keng Lee, Hannah C. Jordan, and Jason Horsley, "Value of Urban Green Spaces in Promoting Healthy Living and Wellbeing: Prospects for Planning," *Risk Management and Healthcare Policy* 27, no. 8 (August 2015): 131–37.

30. "Affordable Homes Act Would Have $25B Economic Benefit Over Five Years | Mass.Gov," accessed February 28, 2024, https://www.mass.gov/news/affordable-homes-act-would-have-25b-economic-benefit-over-five-years.

31. "'Green' Jobs and Skills Development for Disadvantaged Groups," webinar, Community Energy Association (England), October 27, 2022, https://communityenergyengland.org/events/green-jobs-and-skills-development-for-disadvantaged-groups-online-webinar.

32. Carlos Martín, Carolyn Kousky, Manann Donoghoe, and Karina French, "Federal Disaster Management Is a Confusing Patchwork. Reforming FEMA and Improving Interagency Coordination Can Fix It," Brookings, August 3, 2023, https://www.brookings.edu/articles/federal-disaster-management-is-a-confusing-patchwork-reforming-fema-and-improving-interagency-coordination-can-fix-it/.

33. "Environmental Justice Resources for Teachers and Students," California Coastal Commission, accessed February 28, 2024, https://www.coastal.ca.gov/publiced/directory/ejed.html.

34. Andre M. Perry, Joia Crear-Perry, Carl Romer, and Nana Adjeiwaa-Manu, "The Racial Implications of Medical Debt: How Moving Toward Universal Health Care and Other Reforms Can Address Them," Brookings, accessed February 28, 2024, https://www.brookings.edu/articles/the-racial-implications-of-medical-debt-how-moving-toward-universal-health-care-and-other-reforms-can-address-them/.

ACKNOWLEDGMENTS

My adoptive mothers Elsie Boyd and Mary Herndon taught me in word and deed some basic physics of success: accomplishments develop from one form to another and achievements cannot come from nothing or disappear entirely. Simply put: nothing is self-made. The sweetest fruit of our labor is picked by someone else.

I hear, feel, and see my mothers' work and accomplishments with every one of my publications. For my recent policy impacts on housing, education, and health care, I thank the hundreds of researchers and activists who planted a seed. The invaluable contributions of my colleagues, friends, family, and the numerous researchers whose works I have studied yet never had the pleasure to meet have profoundly enriched this book. I will do my best to thank some of them.

To my beloved children Jade, Carlos, and Roby, you prove to me that when you have family you have power. In the most challenging of times, I've come out of the other side stronger. Thank you for being there for me, and it's my honor to be a father to you.

I am privileged to work at the Brookings Institution, where the scholars and the staff's brilliance, quality, and impact shines through in our research, all of which serves the greater purpose of advancing policy and democracy. I hope to represent my division, Brookings Metro, with distinction.

Much of the research in the book was produced in partnership with my friend and writing partner Jonathan Rothwell of Gallup. Jonathan's analytical gifts and insights truly shine throughout the book, and I want to express my heartfelt gratitude for his partnership.

Present and past members of my research team at the Brookings Institution are prominently featured in this text. My assistant director, Anthony Fiano, has expertly managed the complex logistics of research presentations, government hearings, speaking engagements, and media appearances during one of the most challenging periods of my life. His unwavering dedication to our work led to the establishment of the Center for Community Uplift at Brookings, for which I am profoundly grateful. Dinetta Parrot, my development officer, ensures that my aspirations are fully supported. Mannan Donoghoe's research assistance has been invaluable, and his scholarship on climate justice has significantly informed and shaped my research agenda. Additionally, Hannah Stephens ensures that my work on wealth and business growth maintains the highest standards.

This book also bears the influence of numerous researchers and practitioners, including Amy Liu, Carl Romer, Anthony Barr, David Harshbarger, Makada Henry-Nickie, Rashawn Ray, Vanessa Perry, Jordan Fields, Tynesia Boyea-Robinson, Lisa Rice, Darrick Hamilton, Stuart Yasgur, Xavier

Briggs, Yonina Gray, Dan Foy, Jon Clifton, Kristen Broady, Lyneir Richardson, Camille Busette, Tracy Hadden-Loh, Regina Seo, Keon Gilbert, Rich McGahey, Sarah Treuhaft, Nikole Hannah-Jones, Julian Glover, Anika Goss, Chase Cantrell, Orlando Bailey, Tawanna Black, Aria Florant, Antwi Akom, Trabian Shorter, Helene Gayle, Samantha Tweedy, Alaina Beverly, Shaun Gittens, Eden Gaines, Nasir Qadree, Calvin Gladney, Flozell Daniels, Jenny Scheutz, Tiffany Ford, Sheena Collier, Nicole Elam, Angelique Power, Stan Drayton, Darren Hudson, Fletcher Brooks, Darren Sands, Dan Hartley, Aletha Maybank, Rodney Sampson, Rob Maxim, Lynette Rawlings, Derrick Johnson, Yumeka Rushing, Charity Dean, Erica Miles, Toni Griffin, Jackie Priestly, Darrell West, Mark Lopez, Alexis McGill Johnson, LesLeigh Ford, Carol Graham, Szena Dayo, Lachy Roach, and John Legend. Their insights and contributions have profoundly shaped this work.

I have the best agents in the world. Thank you Rolisa Tutwyler of CCMNT Speakers for masterfully managing my speaking engagements and Gail Ross of WME Books for getting the book deal done.

I am profoundly grateful to the Metropolitan editorial team, led by Riva Hocherman, for recognizing the potential in my book idea and for meticulously refining my thoughts and words throughout the process. In addition to Riva's insightful edits, Alex Foster and Chris O'Connell played vital roles in bringing my vision to life. Their contributions were invaluable, and I cannot thank them enough.

There are many others who I have neglected to share my appreciation to. Please accept my commitment to truth and justice as a thank you.

INDEX

ABC13 KTRK (TV station), 179
Abell Foundation, 112
abolitionists, 50, 139–40
Act Like a Lady, Think Like a Man (Harvey), 131
ACT reports, 143
Addo, Fenaba R., 128–29
ADHD, 139
affirmative action, 15–16
African immigrants, 39
Afro-pessimism, 47, 165–66
Afro-Pessimism (Wilderson), 165
air pollution, 31, 32, 46, 47, 192
Alabama, 146, 153–55
Ali, Ahmed, 149
"All Labor Has Dignity" (King), 173, 176–77
Amazon, 85, 149, 168–75
American Airlines, 166
American Community Survey, 100
American dream, 72, 97–98
American JOBS Act (2012), 67
American Lung Association, 192
American Prospect, 171
Amite County, Mississippi, 163
Anarcha (enslaved woman), 154–55

Anderson, James D., 144–45
Annual Business Survey, 75, 78, 83, 87
AP African American studies, 148
Apple corporation, 60
Appraisal Gap from Historic Redlining Financial Assistance Program, 114
Arlington County, Virginia, 41
Asian Americans, 15, 29, 30, 39, 55, 75–77, 88, 110, 142
Association of America Educators, 149
Atlanta, 41
auto industry, 160–62, 166–67, 175–76, 190–92
Aziz, Rasheed, 52–54

Bait (restaurant), 86
Baker County, Florida, 41
Baltimore, 41, 52–57, 65–68, 112–18
Bank of America, 60, 106
  Community Affordable Loan Solution, 106

banks, 18, 22, 91, 94, 98–99, 104, 106
Barnstable County, Massachusetts, 33
Baton Rouge, Louisiana, 145–46
Bennett, Chris, 78, 89
Bessemer, Alabama, 168–70, 174–75
Betsey (enslaved woman), 154–55
Beyoncé, 6, 17
Bezos, Jeff, 169
Bibb County, Alabama, 163
BizNOLA, 152
Black Arts Movement, 1
Black codes, 102
Black credit unions, 116
Black history, 147–48, 153–55
Black Lives Matter, 1–3, 5, 169
Black Panther Party, 3
Black Politics Today, 1
Black power. *See also specific factors*
　business ownership and, 10–11, 14, 18–22, 25–26, 51, 71–95
　capital and, 13
　collective nature of, 4, 8, 26
　commercial property and, 51–70
　community safety and, 25, 43–44
　conflict resolution and, 46
　core dimensions and goals of, 1–8, 14–16
　culture and, 24–25
　discriminatory policy and, 20
　economic empowerment and, 8, 17, 19–20, 24–25
　education and, 12, 14, 139–49, 158–59
　employer firms and, 74–75
　environmental quality and, 14, 25
　family structure and, 12, 14, 25, 46
　health and, 81
　homeownership and, 11, 14, 97, 100, 101
　income and, 13–14
　individualism and, 8, 25–26
　land and, 14, 51
　life expectancy and, 10–12, 16, 23, 28, 32
　localities and, 48
　marriage and family and, 125–26, 131–34
　metrics to assess, 8–10, 23–27
　reparations and, 25–26, 180–99
　unionization and, 160–77
　wealth and, 17–19, 20–21, 23, 24, 81
　well-being and, 23
　white institutions and, 5
Black Power (Ture and Hamilton), 3, 140
Black Progress Index, 10, 12, 31, 33, 36, 40–41, 42, 47, 53–54, 74–75, 96, 141, 162–63, 192
Black Renaissance, 1, 3, 9
Black Wall Street, 9
Black women
　double gap, 123
　medical experiments on, 154–55
Bluest Eye, The (Morrison), 7
book bans, 2, 149, 150
Boston Task Force on Reparations, 180
Breen, Casey, 36–37
Brookings Institution, 2, 42, 78–79, 88–90, 92, 99, 116–19, 122, 133–34
Brooklyn, New York, 117
Browder, Michelle, 154–55
Brown, Dorothy A., 130
brownfields, 184–96
Brown v. Board of Education of Topeka, 7, 145
Buffalo, New York, 166
Buffett, Warren, 73
Building and Loan Associations, 97
Bureau of Labor Statistics, 170

Burwell v. Hobby Lobby Stores, 165
Busette, Camille, 42
Bush, Cori, 181
Bush, George W., 97
business ownership, 14, 17–20,
    23–26, 71–95
  Black Power and, 23–24
  capital and, 89–90, 92–94
  collective mission, 78
  community development and,
    54–62, 67
  education and, 80–81
  expanding, 51, 75, 78–79, 82,
    88–93
  family and, 85
  health and, 81–82
  life expectancy and, 10–11, 34,
    38–39, 74–75
  partnerships and, 79
  racialized risk and, 58
  rates among Blacks and, 31, 74
  wealth and, 21, 81–82
Butler County, Missouri, 163
Butts County, Georgia, 41
Bynum, Lashelle, 65–66, 70

California, 103, 180
Camden Yards (Baltimore), 52–53
Campaign Zero, 2
cancer, 178–79, 185–86, 188–89,
    195
capital, 13, 20, 24, 58, 63–67, 77,
    82, 87–93, 95, 99, 135
capitalism, 10, 18–20
Cardi B, 1
Career Karma, 78, 89
CARES Act (2020), 94
Caribbean Americans, 39
Cass County, North Dakota, 39
Catonsville, Maryland, 66
CBS MoneyWatch, 167
Census Bureau, 31, 34, 45, 83, 88,
    100, 122, 124

Centers for Disease Control and
    Prevention (CDC), 31, 45
Chandra, Anita, 43
Charles County, Maryland, 162–63
Charleston, South Carolina, 50, 73
Charlotte, North Carolina, 106
Chauvin, Derek, 2
Chicago, 61, 62, 83
Chicago TREND, 59–60, 62,
    64–66, 68
childcare centers, 78
children
  incarceration of parent and,
    134–35, 139
  not living with father, 31,
    45–46, 54, 121–36
  pollution and, 178–79, 188
Citywide Youth Development,
    52, 54
civic action, 30, 32, 97, 139,
    198–99
Civil Rights Act
  (1866), 15, 73, 124
  (1964), 15, 186
civil rights movement, 3–4, 48,
    139
Civil War, 3, 13, 49–51, 150
Clarke County, Mississippi, 96
Cleveland, 101
climate change, 193, 198
closing costs, 106, 108
CNN, 103–4
cohabitation, 125, 127–28
collective bargaining, 167, 170, 176
College Board, 143
colleges and universities, 15, 31,
    41, 80–81, 141, 144, 146–47,
    152, 164
Collier County, Florida, 30
Colonial Williamsburg, 65
Comcast, 60
commercial property, 51–52,
    57–64, 117

community development, 57–69, 91, 152–53
Confederacy, 50, 145, 150
Consumer Financial Protection Bureau, 103
Cool Cities Initiative, 194
Cornell University, 127, 128, 165
corporations, 2, 165, 169, 181, 182, 188, 189
Cosby Show, The (TV show), 124–25
Costco, 169
County Health Rankings and Roadmaps, 31
COVID-19, 83, 86, 93–94, 100, 119–22, 168–70, 172
Creative Changemakers Museum, 155
credit, 12, 91, 99, 104–6, 127
crime, 43, 56, 82, 97, 139
criminal justice system, 125, 139
critical race theory (CRT), 147–49
crowdfunding, 60, 62, 67
CROWN Act, 7
Cumberland County, Maine, 33

Dallas, Texas, 106
Dallas County, Iowa, 33
Darity, William A., Jr., "Sandy," 14, 21–22,180–81, 188
de jure segregation, 26–27
Delaware, 146
Delaware County, Ohio, 33
Democratic Party, 30, 103, 150, 181
DeSantis, Ron, 147–48, 150
Detroit, 100, 106, 189–96
Detroit Brownfield Development Association, 194
Detroit Land Bank Authority, 69
Detroit LISC, 194
Detter, Dag, 92
Dewey, John, 157

"Discriminatory Effects of Credit Scoring" (Rice and Swesnik), 104
Douglass, Frederick, 139–40
DuVernay, Ava, 1

Eads, Alicia, 127
East Baton Rouge Parish Public Schools, 146
East Studios LLC, 152
Eberhardt, Peter, 63
economic mobility, 42, 63, 72
Economic Policy Institute, 164, 166
Edmondson Village Shopping Center, 65–70
Edmondson-Westside High School, 66
education, 10, 12–14, 25, 37–42, 80–82, 88–89, 97, 118, 123, 125, 133, 135, 137–59, 164, 181, 188
Education of Blacks in the South, The (Anderson), 144–45
Education Trust, 156–57
Education Week, 147
Elliott, Sharon, 179
Emancipation Proclamation, 49, 139
Emmons, William, 142
employer firms, 22, 51, 54–55, 75–81, 83–85, 87, 91–92, 94
Entrepreneurs Making and Growing Enterprises (EMAGE) Center, 53
Environmental Protection Agency (EPA), 178, 184–88, 190, 193
environmental quality, 14, 16, 25, 29, 31, 46–47, 182, 190, 193–97
Equal Credit Opportunity Act, 105–6
Equal Justice Initiative, 153–54
Equal Protection Clause, 15

Esusu, 90
Evanston, Illinois, 13–14, 180
Expanded Learning Time Initiative,
    156

Facebook, 31, 42
Fain, Shawn, 161
Fairfax County, Virginia, 32, 33
Fair Housing Act (1968), 102–3,
    106
False Black Power (Riley), 26
"Family Feud" (song), 17
Fayetteville, North Carolina, 83
Federal Bureau of Prisons, 134
Federal Emergency Management
    Agency (FEMA), 197
federal government, 22, 181, 188
Federal Reserve, 20, 31, 99, 133–34
FICO 10T, 104–5
Fifth Ward, Houston, 178, 182
First Amendment, 150
Fleming, Cicely, 13–14
Flint, Michigan, 99
Florida, 147–50
Florida Board of Education, 147–48
Florida Education Association, 148
Floyd, George, 1–2, 60–62, 169
Fölster, Stefan, 92
Forbes World Billionaires List, 18
Ford Motors, 160–61, 167,
    190–91
Forschim, Kim, 175–76
Forsythe County, Georgia, 33, 41
Foster, Michael, 171
Fourteenth Amendment, 15
France, 24
Frazier, Garrison, 49–50, 69
Freedmen's Bureau, 13, 144–45
Freedom Farms, 116
Freedom Monument Sculpture
    Park, 153–54
From Here to Equality (Darity and
    Mullen), 180

Frozen Desert Sorbet & Café,
    52–53

Gallup, 47, 75–76, 80, 85
Garza, Alicia, 1
General Motors (GM), 160, 161,
    176
geographic areas, compared,
    29–31, 33, 35, 41, 83, 96–97,
    158, 162–64, 170
Georgia, 27, 83
GI Bill (1944), 133
GigEasy, 90
Glover, Ryan, 9
Government Accountability Office,
    146
Grammy Awards, 4–6
Gray, Freddie, 53
Greenwood mobile banking, 9

Hamer, Fannie Lou, 3
Hamilton, Charles V., 140
Hamilton, Jeremiah, 22
Hancock County, Indiana, 96
Harlem, 117
Harlem Renaissance, 1
Harris, Ruben, 78, 89
Harrison, Toni, 189
Harshbarger, David, 99
Harvard University, 15, 98, 126
Harvey, Steve, 131
Hawaii, 170
health, 10, 35–36, 39–44, 81–86,
    97, 122–23, 138, 141,
    163–64, 189
health care, 11, 20, 30, 28, 35, 37,
    79–80, 82, 84–86, 94, 97, 198
health-care companies, 80–81, 93
health insurance, 20, 39, 171
Henry Ford museum, 190
Hess Shoe Store, 65
Hicks, Jeffrey, 118
Hidalgo County, Texas, 38

Hispanic Americans (Latinos), 11,
     30, 63, 75–77, 84, 88, 90,
     98–99, 103, 110–11, 133,
     142, 188
historically Black colleges and
     universities (HBCUs), 146, 152
Hochschild, Kohn & Co., 65
Hodgest, Kalen, 71–72, 76, 78–80,
     85–88, 95
Holder, Michelle, 123
homeownership, 4–5, 8, 10–12,
     14, 20–21, 24, 34, 36–38, 54,
     96–119, 123, 126, 187, 196
Homeownership Council of
     America, 105, 107–10
Home Owners' Loan Corporation
     Act (1933), 102
Homestead Act (1862), 102
Hoover, Herbert, 97
HOPE Village Revitalization
     project, 193–95
housing, 20, 28, 36–37, 54–57,
     94, 98–101, 111–12, 119,
     125, 133, 135, 149, 181, 183,
     191–92, 194, 196
Housing and Urban Development
     Department, 106
housing equity, 84, 99, 100
housing grants, 14
housing markets, 98, 101, 111
housing organizations, 102
housing policies, 29, 102–3, 133,
     185–86
housing values, 8, 98–99, 197
Houston, Texas, 14, 100, 178–80,
     182, 186–89
Houston Public Media, 187
Howard County, Maryland, 41
How Capitalism Underdeveloped
     Black America (Marable), 18
"How Social Networks Impact
     Economic Mobility"
     (Busette), 42

Idaho House of Representatives,
     147
Ignite Capital, 115
Illinois, 190
incarceration, 12, 45, 125, 133–35,
     137, 139, 171
income, 13, 21, 31, 34, 35, 40,
     100, 111–12, 123, 125, 134,
     141–43, 160–77
  basic, 163
Indianapolis, 8
infrastructure, 20, 29, 185–86
Internal Revenue Service (IRS), 31,
     130, 134
investment, 24, 44, 54–68, 89,
     91–92, 99. See also business
     ownership; capital

Jackson, Mississippi, 42–43
Jacksonville, Florida, 7–8, 41
Jasper County, Mississippi, 96
Jay-Z, 6, 17, 19
Jefferson County, Ohio, 30
Jim Crow, 36, 73–74, 102, 140,
     145, 183
jobs, 55, 59, 84, 87, 91, 125, 191,
     193, 195–97
job stability, 171
Johns Hopkins University, 54, 115
Jones, Bree, 112–18
Jones, Hannah, 111
Jones, Shevrin, 150
Jordan, Michael B., 1
Journal of Exposure Science &
     Environmental Epidemiology,
     192
Journal of Marriage and Family,
     128–29
Journal of Social Sciences, 127
Journal of the American Medical
     Association, 34
Journal of Urbanism, 81–82
JPMorgan Chase, 115

Kaepernick, Colin, 19
Katrina, Hurricane, 99, 151
Kemp, Brian, 27
Kendi, Ibram X., 1, 3, 9
Killer Mike, 9
King, Martin Luther, Jr., 3, 28–29, 173, 176–77
King, Regina, 9
Known company, 90–91
Ku Klux Klan, 191

Labor Department, 132
Labor Notes, 175
labor unions, 13, 160–62, 166–77
landlords, 19, 56–57, 90
landownership, 14, 49–51, 102, 114
Landry, Jeff, 186
Lasso algorithm, 31
Learning Policy Institute, 156
Le Code Noir, 24
Legacy Museum, 153–54
Legacy Sites, 153–54
Leidesdorff, William Alexander, 22
libraries, 156, 158
Lichter, Daniel T., 128–29
life expectancy, 28–48
    air pollution and, 31, 46, 192
    Blacks and, vs. other groups, 28–30
    business ownership and, 10–11, 31, 38–39, 74–75
    children not living with father and, 31, 45–46, 122
    church membership and, 31, 42–43
    community safety and, 31, 43–44
    commuting and, 31
    discrimination and, 44
    disparities among Black populations, 10
    education and, 12–13, 31, 40–41, 141
    Facebook Friends and, 31, 42

factors most affecting, 31–32
    as first metric of Black Power, 10, 16
    foreign-born Blacks and, 31, 38–39
    geography and, 10–11, 29–32, 33, 41, 48
    health and, 39–40
    homeownership and, 11–12, 31, 36–38, 96–97
    income and, 13, 31, 162–68
    individual behavior and, 35–36
    ownership and, 10
    population density and, 31, 46–47
    wealth and, 34–35
    well-being and, 23
Lincoln, Abraham, 49–50
literacy, 41, 140, 143
Living Wage Institute, 173–74
local governments, 13–14, 69, 178–82, 188–89
Loh, Tracy Hadden, 51, 116
Los Angeles, 106, 108
Loudoun County, Virginia, 33, 41, 162
Louisiana, 24, 111, 137–38, 146, 185–86
Louisiana Budget Project, 138
Louisiana Purchase, 24
Louisiana Supreme Court, 145
Love, Hanna, 116–17
Loving v. Virginia, 124
low-income housing, 82, 87, 115–16, 188
low-income housing tax credits (LIHTC), 61
Lucy (enslaved woman), 154–55
lynching, 154

Mackie, Anthony, 152–53
Mackie, Calvin, 137, 151–53, 157
Made in B'more apparel, 52–53
Mahool, J. Barry, 68

Malcolm X, 3
Manassas Park, Virginia, 30
manufacturing, 18, 93, 190
Marable, Manning, 18, 19
marriage, 12, 120–36
Martin Luther King Jr. Day, 74
Marvel, 152
Maryland, 68, 114, 162–163
Massachusetts, 156, 180
Mathews, Pamela, 188–89
math proficiency, 31, 54, 142–43,
    156–57
McKinsey firm, 2
Medicaid, 81
Medicare, 39
Memphis, 100
    sanitation strike, 28, 173
Meyerhoff, Jacob, 65–66
Meyerhoff, Joseph, 65–66
Miami, Florida, 78, 106
Michigan, 189–90, 193–94
minimum wage laws, 164,
    173–74
Minneapolis, 39, 60, 169
Minnesota, 190
Missouri, 81, 181
Moller, Jan, 138
Montgomery, Alabama, 153–54
Montgomery County, Maryland,
    30, 33, 34, 53
More Up Travel Center, 155
Morrison, Toni, 7
Mortgage Bankers Association,
    107
mortgages, 20, 38, 91, 98–110,
    119, 127, 133
Mothers of Gynecology Health and
    Wellness Clinic, 155
Mothers of Gynecology
    monument, 154–55
Moynihan, Daniel Patrick, 35,
    132–33
Mullen, A. Kirsten, 14, 180–81, 188

NAACP, 10, 148
*Narrative of the Life of Frederick
    Douglass* (Douglass), 140
Nash, Don, 105–6, 108–10
Nassau County, New York, 33
National Assessment of Education
    Progress (NAEP), 142–43, 150
National Association of Real Estate
    Brokers, 118
National Association of Realtors
    (NAR), 111–12
National Fair Housing Alliance
    (NFHA), 104, 107
National Housing Act (1934), 102
National Interstate and Defense
    Highways Act (1956), 102–3
National Labor Relations Board
    (NLRB), 171, 175
National Memorial for Peace and
    Justice, 153–54
Native Americans, 29, 75, 90, 181,
    185
Navy Federal Credit Union, 103, 104
Negro Family, The (Moynihan), 35,
    132–33
New Deal, 101
New Economics Foundation, 23
New Kent County, Virginia, 96
New Orleans, 24–25, 73, 94–95,
    137–38, 151–53, 198
New York City, 83
New York State, 170
New York Times, 7–8, 21–22, 25
NFL, 19
Nike, 60
Nixon, Richard, 19–20
North Carolina, 22
nutrition, 37, 40, 43

Obama, Barack, 97–98
obesity, 36, 42, 44
Office of Policy Planning and
    Research, 132

Ogbu, John, 39
Ohio, 146, 190
Oscars, 4
ownership, 9–10, 13. *See also*
    business ownership;
    homeownership;
    landownership
ozone, 192–93

Parity Homes, 112–18
Path to 15/55 collaborative, 91–92
Paycheck Protection Program
    (PPP), 94
Pearson, Bill, 104
PEN America, 2, 149
Pew Research Center, 45, 111
philanthropy, 53, 61, 64–65, 115,
    169
plantations, 29, 185
police, 2, 19, 44, 53, 60
pollution, 14, 43, 135, 178–79,
    182–98. *See also* brownfields
population density, 31, 46–47
Porter, Billy, 9
poverty, 35–36, 44, 100, 125–26,
    135, 138
presidential election of 2020, 26,
    146–47
Prince George's County, Maryland,
    32, 34, 36, 38, 41–45, 47, 53
Prince William County, Virginia, 33
Prison Policy Initiative (PPI),
    137–38
Public Wealth of Cities (Detter and
    Fölster), 92
Putnam County, New York, 33

racial discrimination and racism,
    6–7, 13. *See also* Jim Crow;
    segregation
  American society and, 47
  business ownership and, 22
  collective initiatives to address, 116

criminal justice and, 44, 125, 139
denial of, by whites, 150
education and, 140, 146–51,
    181–82
employer firms and, 77
environmental quality and, 46,
    193, 196–97
homeownership and, 101–5,
    181–82
housing and, 20, 36–37, 98–99,
    133, 135, 149, 181, 183
HVAC systems and, 196
individual behavior and, 36
industrial profits and, 18
infrastructure and, 46
jobs and, 125, 191, 193
life expectancy and, 30
markets and, 77
marriage and, 126, 131–33
minimizing risk assumed by, 58
power of Black wealth and, 23
racial wealth gap and, 25
redress for, 25, 181
religion and, 43
reparations and, 14, 181–82
sexism and, 135–36
whites enriched by, 24
racial wealth gap, 13, 21–22, 25,
    40, 51, 62–63, 100, 110, 181,
    197
Rae, Issa, 9
Ray, Rashawn, 2
Reagan, Ronald, 97
real estate development, 10–11,
    59–68, 85–87
real estate investment trusts
    (REITs), 117
Realtor.com, 111
Reconstruction, 74, 144–45, 148
Recording Academy, 6
Redfin, 31
redlining, 36, 98–99, 133, 192, 198
religion, 25, 42–43

renters, 56, 100–102, 118, 187
reparations, 13–15, 20, 25, 49–51,
    178–99
  defining, 183–84
  environmental injustice and, 14,
    178–80, 184–99
  federal, 14, 180–82
  local, 13–14, 178–80
  state, 180
Republican Party, 26, 30, 50, 147,
    148–49
restrictive covenants, 67–69, 98, 102
Retail, Wholesale and Department
    Store Union (RWDSU), 168,
    171–72, 175
retirement funds, 91, 171
Reynolds, Jason, 9
Rice, Lisa, 104, 107
Richardson, Lyneir, 59–70
Ricketts, Lowell, 142
right-to-work laws, 170
Rihanna, 89
Riley, Jason L., 26, 27
risk, 58, 92
Riverfront Times, 86
Rockingham County, New
    Hampshire, 33
Rothwell, Jonathan, 10, 51, 55, 99
Russonello, Giovanni, 25

safety, 10, 25, 28–29, 31, 37, 40, 138
SAG-AFTRA strike, 109
Samuels, Kevin, 132
Saratoga County, New York, 33
Savage X Fenty, 89
Savannah, 73
Schneider, Daniel, 126–27
schools, 2, 27–28, 39, 41, 138–39,
    197–98
  CRT and, 147–49
  extended learning time and,
    156–57
  segregation of, 144–47

Scott County, Minnesota, 33, 39
Seaborn, Henry and Charlotte,
    130
Securities and Exchange
    Commission, 67
segregation, 26–27
  auto plants and, 191
  education and, 144–47, 150
  housing and, 29, 67–68, 98, 99,
    104, 180, 185–86, 191–92
  Legacy Sites and history of,
    154
  marriage and, 133
  occupational, 173
  reparations and, 14, 183
self-employment, 81, 85, 165
"separate but equal," 7, 145
7th Inning Sorbet, 52
sexism, 125, 131, 135–36
Sharecare, 47
Shark Tank (TV show), 89
Sherman, William T., 49–51
Silicon Valley, 89
Sims, J. Marion, 154–55
single-parent households, 121–23,
    125, 174
slavery, 18
  abolition of, 145
  anti-literacy and, 145
  Black history and, 148
  descendants of, vs. foreign-born
    Blacks, 39
  education and, 140, 144–45, 150
  entrepreneurship and 22, 24–25,
    73–74
  environmental degradation and,
    29, 185
  historic impact of, 165
  homeownership and, 36
  involuntary minorities and, 39
  Legacy Sites and, 154
  marriage and, 132–33
  Massachusetts and, 180

medical experiments and, 154–55
New Orleans and, 24–25
reparations and, 3, 13–14, 22, 25, 180–83, 199
SmallChange.co platform, 67
Smith family, 109, 110
Snohomish County, Washington, 33
social networks, 25, 42–43, 97
South, 83, 144–46, 170, 175
Spar, Andrew, 148
SPCPs, 105–10, 119
Stanford Center for Racial Justice, 15
Stanly, John Carruthers, 22–23
Stanton, Edwin M., 49
Starbucks, 166
state governments, 22, 26–27, 69, 105, 147–49, 173, 181–82
State of the Air report, 192
Stellantis, 160–61
STEM NOLA, 137, 151–53
Stevens, Thaddeus, 50
Stevenson, Bryan, 153–54
St. Johns River, Florida, 50
St. Louis, Missouri, 71, 79, 83, 85–87, 89, 91, 93, 95, 100, 176
"Stop WOKE Act" (Florida), 147
Stout, Lynn, 165
Students for Fair Admissions, Inc. v. President and Fellows of Harvard College, 15–16
Sumner, Charles, 50
Survey of Consumer Finances, 99
Swesnik, Deidre, 104
Syracuse University, 167

Tach, Laura, 127
Task Force to Study and Develop Reparations Proposals, 180
taxes, 20, 24, 57, 59, 69, 102, 113–15, 118, 123, 130–31, 193–94

Tennessee, 146
Tesla, 161
Texas, 186
Thirteenth Amendment (1865), 73, 124
Thompson, JC, 168
Time, 1, 9
Title VI, 15
Title VII, 15
Toldson, Ivory, 148
Toyota, 161
TREND CDC, 64–65
Truly Disadvantaged, The (Wilson), 125
Trump, Donald, 26, 147
Tulsa, Oklahoma, 9
Ture, Kwame, 3, 140
Turner, Nicholas, 133–34
Turner, Sylvester, 179, 189

Union Army, 49
Union Pacific, 178–79, 182, 188–89
United Auto Workers (UAW), 160–61, 166–67
United Nations, 182–85
University of California, 165–66
University of Chicago, 46
University of Maryland, 116
University of North Carolina, 15, 128
Urban Institute, 110
Urban Wealth Funds, 92
US Congress, 103, 130, 180–81, 197
    Joint Economic Committee, Social Capital Project, 31
US Constitution, 4, 102
US House of Representatives
    Financial Services Committee, 103
    Judiciary Committee, 181
    Resolution 40, 181

US Supreme Court, 7, 15–16, 124, 145, 165, 186

VantageScore 4.0, 104–5
venture capital, 89–91
Veterans Administration, 71
Vice News, 168
Vincent, Lynne, 167
voting rights, 3, 26–27, 139

wages, 91, 160–77. *See also* income; wealth
  living, 9, 14, 28, 173–77
Walker, Madam C. J., 22
Walmart, 169
Walt Disney World, 166
Ward, Jesmyn, 1
War on Drugs, 133
Warrick County, Indiana, 33
Washington, DC, 41, 111, 117
Washington Center for Equitable Growth, 123
Washington County, Oregon, 33
Washington Post, 14
Washington University, 89
Waters, Maxine, 103
wealth, 10–13, 17–18, 20–21, 23–24, 31, 34–35, 37–38, 57, 76–77, 81–82, 84, 97, 99–100, 111, 122–29, 131, 133–36, 142–44, 155, 162, 185. *See also* income; racial wealth gap; wages
Wekker, Gloria, 6
Weld County, Colorado, 30
well-being, 16, 27, 36, 57, 63, 138
  life expectancy and, 10, 23
Wentzville Assembly Center, 176
white flight, 66, 103, 192
Whiteness of Wealth, The (Brown), 130

white norming, 5–9
whites
  business ownership and, 51, 55–56, 75–77, 84, 88, 99
  education and, 150
  family and, 135
  homeownership and, 11, 36, 98–99
  landownership and, 50
  life expectancy and, 29–30
  middle class and, 20
  wealth and, 77, 99, 111, 135
  willful ignorance and, 150–51
white suburbs, 185–86
white supremacy, 5, 135, 141, 149
whitewashing, 7–8
Wial, Howard, 63
Wilcox, W. Bradford, 127–28
Wilderson, Frank B., III, 165
Williams, Stephen, 178
Wilson, William Julius, 125
Wire, The (TV show), 53
Wisconsin, 190
WMAR Channel 2, 70
Wonderschool, 78, 89
World War I, 190–91
Wright County, Minnesota, 33, 162
Writers Guild of America, 108–9

Xavier University, 152

Yale Law School, 68
Yellen, Janet, 74
Yelp, 55–56, 88
Young, Andrew, Jr., 9

Zeal Capital, 90–91
Zillow, 100
zoning, 64, 98, 101–2, 179